P-Prolog
A Parallel Logic Programming Language

World Scientific Series in Computer Science

Volume 1: Computer-aided Specification Techniques
by J Demetrovics, E Knuth & P Rado

Volume 2: Proceedings of the 2nd RIKEN International Symposium on Symbolic and Algebraic Computation by Computers
edited by N Inada & T Soma

Volume 3: Computational Studies of the Most Frequent Chinese Words and Sounds
by Ching Y Suen

Volume 4: Understanding and Learning Statistics by Computer
by M C K Yang & D H Robinson

Volume 6: DC Flux Parametron
A New Approach to Josephson Junction Logic
by E Goto & K F Loe

Volume 8: Information, Randomness & Incompleteness –
Papers on Algorithmic Information Theory
by G J Chaitin

Volume 9: P-Prolog – A Parallel Logic Programming Language
by Rong Yang

Forthcoming titles:

Volume 5: Information Control Problems in Manufacturing Automation
by L Nemes

Volume 7: Syntactic and Structural Pattern Recognition –
Fundamentals, Advances and Applications
edited by H Bunke & A Sanfeliu

Series in Computer Science — Vol. 9

P-Prolog
A Parallel Logic Programming Language

Rong Yang

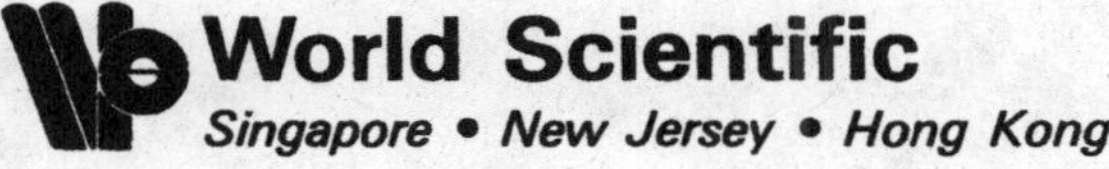

Published by

World Scientific Publishing Co. Pte. Ltd.
P.O. Box 128, Farrer Road, Singapore 9128

U. S. A. office: **World Scientific Publishing Co., Inc.**
687 Hartwell Street, Teaneck NJ 07666, USA

Library of Congress Cataloging-in-Publication data is available.

P-PROLOG – A PARALLEL LOGIC PROGRAMMING LANGUAGE

ISBN 9971-50-508-8

Printed in Singapore by General Printing and Publishing Services Pte. Ltd.

Acknowledgments

This work was based on the research for my Ph.D. degree at Keio University. I would like to express my gratitude to the following people, who have given much help, advice, encouragement and criticism in this work.

First of all, I am deeply indebted to my advisor professor Hideo Aiso. He introduced me to 5th generation computer science and logic programming languages, and since then he has been providing a warm research enviornment for me. I felt that no student could have had more untiring support, advice and encouragement from an excellent professor than I have had from him.

I am also grateful to professor Mario Tokoro. His suggestions and criticism have been my primary source of inspiration and direction over the years.

I will remain indebted to professor Shoji Ura, professor Kenichi Harada and professor Nobuo Saito, the other members of my degree committee for their comments and suggestions.

I would like to thank Hideharu Amano, Jun Miyazaki, Michio Isoda, Takaichi Yoshida, Yutaka Ishikawa, Hideki Sunahara, Yutaka Akiyama, Takeo Maruichi and Kunihito Matsumura, who are my colleagues at Aiso Lab. and Tokoro Lab. in the Dept. of E.E., Keio Univ., for many interesting hours of discussion. I am especially grateful to Yasuro Shobatake, Toshiki Kikuchi and Hideo Tamura who partly joined my research. Yasuro Shobatake designed a hardware of BTM, Toshiki Kikuchi implemented the kernel of the P-Prolog system with me. And Hideo Tamura implemented P-Prolog's debug system. Their excellent work helped me a lot. I also would like to thank Hideharu Amano, Michio Isoda, Yasuro Shobatake and Kunihito Matsumura for their comments on the first version of this monograph.

In particular, I would like to extend my thanks to Steve Gregory. It was Steve who encouraged and helped me at the most difficult moments of this monograph writing. He taught me the meaning of courage and helped me rediscover it on the several occasions when I lost it. Although he was terribly busy in his work, he spent uncountable weekends to read and improve all of the chapters with a great attention. Many valuable comments, detailed suggestions and criticism from him greatly benefited this monograph.

While revising this monograph, I also obtained many valuable and detailed comments from professor David Warren. I would like to thank him deeply.

I must thank the Setsutaro Kobayashi Memorial Foundation Office of Fuji-Xerox Company, Aiso Lab. and Chinese Education Department which provided me a variety of scholarships during my Ph.D. program.

Finally, I must especially thank my husband, Xiao-ning. His unfailing love sustained me through long years of separation. Without his encouragement and understanding, this research would not have been possible.

Preface

This monograph presents a parallel logic programming language named P-Prolog, and discusses its implementation.

To date, two main research areas for parallel logic programming have been studied:

1. To develop methods, or control strategies, for executing pure Horn clause programs in parallel.
2. To develop new parallel languages based on guarded Horn clauses, and implementation methods for them.

For (1), it is likely that to execute pure Horn clause programs with both *and-parallelism* and *or-parallelism* is quite difficult, so restrictions are usually imposed. The drawback with (2) is that guarded Horn clause languages sacrifice completeness, because they do not incorporate *don't-know non-determinism.*

This monograph presents an alternative proposal, P-Prolog, which provides the advantages of guarded Horn clauses while retaining *don't-know non-determinism* where required. P-Prolog programs are composed of a kind of extended guarded Horn clauses called *classified Horn clauses* which are introduced in this monograph. A novel concept introduced in *classified Horn clauses* is the exclusive relation of guarded Horn clauses. Two advantages resulting from the introduction of *classified Horn clauses* are:

1. The language combines *and-parallelism* and *or-parallelism.* Therefore the execution of P-Prolog can incorporate both *don't-care non-determinism* and *don't-know non-determinism.*
2. The input/output pattern of predicates need not be fixed. Its synchronization mechanism allows the direction of data flow to be determined dynamically.

In terms of implementation, combining *and-* and *or-* parallelism is regarded as a difficult subject. This monograph presents an or-tree model and an implementation scheme for it, to combine these kinds of parallelism with reasonable efficiency. The model and implementation scheme discussed in this monograph can be applied not only to P-Prolog, but also to other parallel logic languages.

This monograph is divided into two parts: language and implementation. In Part I, a brief review of the theory of logic programming and a survey of parallel logic languages are first given; then the concepts, syntax, semantics and characteristics of P-Prolog are described. In Part II, the three main problems of implementation are discussed: representation of data, management of multiple environments and communication between and-process and or-processes.

Contents

Chapter 1

Introduction

1.1 Background

Logic programming languages have been regarded as remarkable in describing parallelism simply and naturally. This is because in logic programming languages a program is treated as a set of assumptions. Just as *A and (or) B* is equivalent to *B and (or) A*, there is no sequence between the assumptions. When a conclusion is derived from the assumptions, we can try to draw the conclusion from different assumptions in parallel (called *or-parallelism*), and also can divide the conclusion into several sub-conclusions to prove them in parallel (called *and-parallelism*). In this sense, logic programming languages can be executed in parallel without any extra parallel syntactic constructs. However, in many cases the sequence of execution affects efficiency very much. Simply evaluating in parallel may cause a lot of redundant processing. For this reason, it is necessary to investigate efficient parallel control strategies and special parallel logic programming languages.

In numerical computation, the most important problems for parallel processing are synchronization and communication. Likewise, parallel logic programming is also facing these two problems in some sense.

1. For the former, (synchronization)

   the existing representative parallel logic languages introduce some syntactic constructs as a synchronization mechanism. Even though these syntactic constructs are different, they have a common purpose: to declare the input/output (I/O for short) pattern of arguments directly or indirectly. Since the I/O pattern is explicit, we can know which processes can be executed and which processes should be suspended to wait for data.

2. For the latter, (communication)

   namely, the communication problem, variables shared by several processes play the role of communication channel in logic programming languages. It is no problem when only *and-parallelism* or *or-parallelism* are executed. But it needs very complicated communication mechanism and environment management when *and-parallelism* and *or-parallelism* are combined with each other.

1.2 Target

The targets of our approach are briefly described as following:

1. We want to find a synchronization mechanism in which the I/O pattern need not be fixed and declared.
2. We want to find a reasonably efficient implementation method to combine *and*- and *or*- parallelism.

1.3 Outline

This dissertation comprises two main parts: language and implementation.

Part one is from Chapter 2 to Chapter 4. Chapter 2 gives a brief review of the theory of logic programming. The essential definitions and the important theories are summarized in this chapter. Chapter 3 is a survey of parallel logic programming languages. Chapter 4 presents a novel parallel logic programming language named P-Prolog which is the main result of our research. In this chapter, the syntax and semantics, language characteristics and programming methodology are described in detail.

Part two is from Chapter 5 to Chapter 7. Three problems relating to implementation of logic programming languages are discussed separately. The first problem that interests us concerns data representation. Chapter 5 proposes a binary tree expression for structured data in order to access data efficiently. The second problem is how to manage multiple environments for ***or-parallelism.*** Chapter 6 gives a survey of this field, and presents two new binding schemes. The third problem is how to combine ***and-parallelism*** and ***or-parallelism*** which is of great interest now. Chapter 7 discusses an execution model for this combining and its implementation scheme which is being used in a prototype implementation of P-Prolog. Though methods proposed in Part two are used for P-Prolog's implementation, the discussion in Chapter 5 is applicable to any logic programming language, the discussion in Chapter 6 is applicable to other ***or-parallel*** languages, and the discussion in Chapter 7 is also applicable to other languages which attempt to combine and- and or- parallelism.

Finally, the work is concluded by Chapter 8, which also mentions future research on P-Prolog.

Part I

LANGUAGE

Chapter 2

Theory of Logic Programming

Logic programming is based on the *resolution principle* [Robinson 65], which is a mechanical inference method applied to *first order logic* . For this reason, we first briefly introduce *first order logic* and the *resolution principle* in this chapter to make this dissertation self-contained. The main references are [Monk 76] [Chang and Lee 73] [Kowalski 79].

2.1 First Order Logic

Logic is a fundamental tool for human thought and action. First order logic is an important branch of logic. It studies and represents implication between assumptions and conclusions. When the assumptions are symbolized into formulas of first order logic, we can use its inference rules to obtain the conclusions from the assumptions. For example, the statements

Mary is a Ph.D student
Tom is not a Ph.D student
A graduate student must write thesis
Every Ph.D student is also called a graduate student

can be symbolized into formulas of first order logic as follows:

A1.1 phd_student(mary)

A1.2 ¬phd_student(tom)

A1.3 (∀x)(must_write_thesis(x) ←g_student(x))

A1.4 (∀x)(g_student(x) ←phd_student(x))

Then a conclusion such that

Mary must write thesis,

namely,

must_write_thesis(mary)

can be obtained by reasoning form **A1.1-A1.4**.

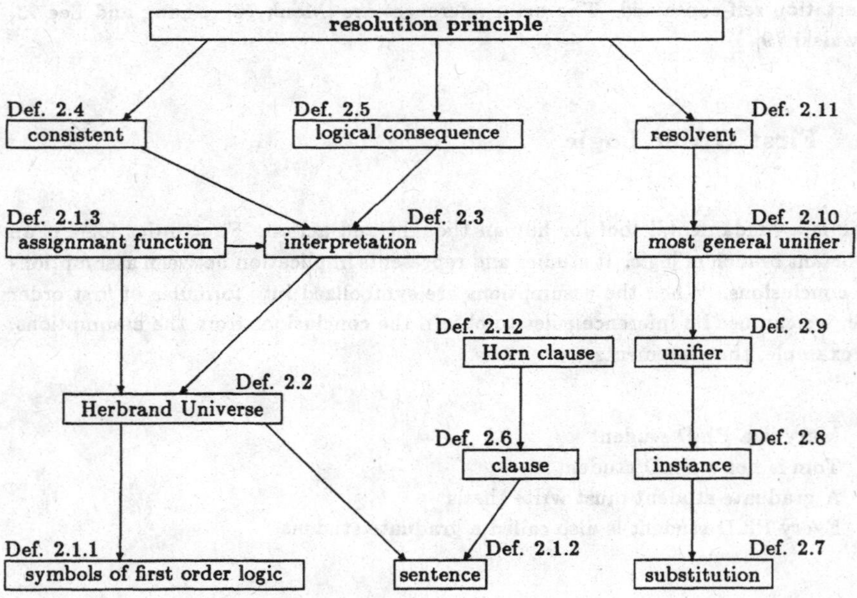

Figure 2.1 Relationship Between Definitions in Chapter 2

In this chapter, we will give some definitions which relate to essential concepts of logic programming. The relationship between these definitions is made explicit in Figure 2.1.

First, some definitions about first order logic are summarized.

Definition 2.1 *First order logic* is a language **L** = < *S1,S2,S3* >, where *S1* is a set of symbols(words), *S2* is syntax, and *S3* is semantics.

1. *S1* includes six kind of symbols: predicate, functor, constant, variable, logic operator ($\neg, \wedge, \vee, \leftarrow, \leftrightarrow$) and quantifier($\forall, \exists$).

2. *S2* gives a set of syntax rules of **L**. A *sentence* of **L** is defined below:

   A *sentence* is a certain kind of *formula* in which all occurrences of a variable must be inside the scope of a quantifier.
   A *formula* is defined as follows:

   < *formula* > ::= < *atomic formula* > |
   ¬< *formula* > |
   < *formula* >∧< *formula* > |
   < *formula* >∨< *formula* > |
   < *formula* > ←< *formula* > |
   < *formula* > ↔< *formula* > |
   (∀x)< *formula* > |
   (∃x)< *formula* >
   (here, **x** is a variable whose occurrences are not within the scope of any quantifiers of the formula)
   < *atomic formula* > ::= predicate (< *term* >, ..., < *term* >)|

   < *term* > ::= variable|constant| functor (< *term* >, ..., < *term* >)

3. *S3* is a function f_I for assigning a truth value to sentences of **L**. For any set of sentences, we can give it some interpretations (see Def. 2.3) to assume which predicate is true. Depending on the interpretation I, f_I is defined as follows:

   The domain of f_I is {1,0} (1 for true, 0 for false).

   For a predicate G f_I (G) = 1 iff G is true in I

f_I (¬G) = 1 iff f_I (G) = 0

f_I (G∧H) = 1 iff f_I (G) = 1 and f_I (H) = 1

f_I (G∨H) = 1 iff f_I (G) = 1 or f_I (H) =1

f_I (G←H) = 1 iff f_I (G) = 1 or f_I (H) = 0

f_I (G↔H) = 1 iff f_I (G) = f_I (H)

f_I ((∀x)(G(x))) = 1 iff for every d in L's Herbrand universe (see Def. 2.2) f_I (G(d)) = 1

f_I ((∃x)(G(x))) = 1 iff at least one d in L's Herbrand universe (see Def. 2.2) f_I (G(d)) = 1

In the above definition there are two words, *Herbrand universe* and *interpretation*, which are important concepts.

Definition 2.2 Let H_0 be the set of constants appearing in a set of sentences S. If no constant appears in S then H_0 is to consist of a single constant, say H_0 = {a}. For i = 0,1,2,..., let H_{i+1} be the union of H_i and the set of all terms of the form f(t_1,...t_n) for all n-place functions f occurring in S, where t_j, j=1,...,n, are members of the set H_i. Then each H_i is called the i-level constants set of S, and H_∞ is called the *Herbrand universe* of S [Chang and Lee 73].

The assumptions A1.1-A1.4 are a simple example for explaining Def. 2.2. They have a finite Herbrand universe, consisting of only two constant symbols

{ mary, tom }.

Since there is no functor in A1.1-A1.4, their Herbrand universe is finite. Here, we give another example which has an infinite Herbrand universe. The following two sentences express the addition rule:

A2.1 (∀x)(plus(0,x,x))

A2.2 (∀xyz)(plus(s(x),y,s(z)) ← plus(x,y,z))

The Herbrand universe of them is

{ 0, s(0), s(s(0)), s(s(s(0))), ... }

Definition 2.3 For a set of sentences S, a *interpretation* I of S is an assignment to predicates occurring in S as follows:

For every *n*-place predicate p,

1. **we choose *n* elements from S's Herbrand universe $t_1, ...t_n$,**

2. **then assign $p(t_1, ..., t_n)$ a truth value: true or false.**

For example, the set of sentences A1.1 - A1.4 has 64 (4^3) interpretations. This is because it has three different predicates and each predicate has four possible values (see Figure 2.2).

	phd_student(X)		graduate_student(X)		must_write_thesis(X)	
	X = mary	X = tom	X = mary	X = tom	X = mary	X = tom
I_0	0	0	0	0	0	0
I_1	0	0	0	0	0	1
.						
.						
.						
I_{42}	1	0	1	0	1	0
I_{43}	1	0	1	0	1	1
.						
.						
.						
I_{47}	1	0	1	1	1	1
.						
.						
.						
I_{63}	1	1	1	1	1	1

(I_{42}, I_{43} and I_{47} can make A1.1-A1.4 true)

Figure 2.2 Interpretations of A1.1-A1.4

2.2 Resolution Principle

Section 2.1 gave an outline of the nature of first order logic; this section explains how one can reason in first order logic.

Definition 2.4 A set of sentences S is *consistent* iff all its sentences are true in some interpretation of S. S is *inconsistent* iff S is not consistent.

The example shown in Figure 2.2 only has three interpretations in which all of A1.1 - A1.4 are true.

Definition 2.5 A sentence G is a *logical consequence* of sentences F1,F2,...,Fn iff for every interpreter I, if F1 ... Fn is true in I, G is also true in I.

When we want to prove a conclusion C is implied by a set of assumptions A, we usually use a refutation method to prove that ($\neg C \wedge A$) is a contradiction. The *resolution principle* is just founded on this refutation method. The essential idea of the *resolution principle* is to add the negation of the conclusions to the set of assumptions and check whether or not it is inconsistent.

Before describing the *resolution principle*, a certain kind of sentence, *clause* , applied by the *resolution principle* must be defined.

Definition 2.6 A *clause* is a special form of sentence which only uses $\vee$ to connect *literals*:

$$< clause > ::= \square \mid < literal > \mid < literal > \vee < clause >$$

$$< literal > ::= < atomic\ formula > \mid \neg < atomic\ formula >$$

[Kowalski 79] [Nilsson 80] etc., show how to convert a sentence to a set of clauses. **For example, the sentences written in A1.1 - A1.4 can be converted into the following clauses:**

{ phd_student(mary), ¬phd_student(tom),

¬g_student(x)∨must_write_thesis(x),

¬phd_student(x)∨g_student(x) }

The relation between the clauses in the set is *and* (∧ operator).

A special case of clause, namely □, is called the *empty clause.* Because the empty clause has no atomic formula that can be true in any interpretation, it is always false. As a result, a set of clauses that includes the empty clause □is inconsistent.

Next, the concepts of substitution and unification are introduced.

Definition 2.7 A *substitution* is a finite set of the form

$$s = \{ x_1 = t_1, ..., x_n = t_n\}$$

where every x_i is a variable, every t_i is a term, and no two x_i and x_j ($1\leq i, j\leq n, i\neq j$) are the same variable.

Definition 2.8 If E is an expression (term or formula), and s = $\{ x_1 = t_1, ..., x_n = t_n\}$ is a substitution, then (E)s is a new expression which is identical to E except that every occurrence of x_i in E is replaced by the term t_i (i = 1, ..., n). (E)s is called an *instance* of E.

Definition 2.9 A substitution s is called a *unifier* for a set $\{E_1, ..., E_n\}$ iff (E_1)s = (E_2)s =...= (E_n)s.

Definition 2.10 A unifier s for a set of clauses $C_1, ..., C_n$ is a *most general unifier* iff it makes the least specific assignment of terms to variables among all unifiers.

Now we give a definition of *resolvent* which is a key concept of resolution.

Definition 2.11 For any two clauses C1 and C2, if there is an atomic formula A in C1 whose complement ¬A' is in C2, and s is a most general unifier of A and A', then (B1 ∨ B2)s is a resolvent of C1 and C2, where B1 and B2 are the clauses remaining after deleting A and A' from C1 and C2 respectively.

Theorem (resolution principle): Given two clauses C1 and C2, a resolvent of C1 and C2 is a logical consequence of C1 and C2. (Refer to [Chang and Lee 73] for its proof.)

Based on this theorem, we have the following mechanical method to reason whether or not a set of clauses S is inconsistent.

1. find a pair of clauses which can be resolved to obtain a resolvent R,
2. if R is □ then stop, else add R to S, go to (1).

If the above procedure can stop at (2), it shows that S is inconsistent. The reasons are as follows:

1. according to Definition 2.4 and 2.5, adding a consequence of S to S does not affect the consistency (or inconsistency),
2. □ is inconsistent.

It can be proved that the resolution algorithm described above is complete, that is, it can stop provided that S is inconsistent.

Example: if we want to prove that must_write_thesis(mary) is a conclusion of A1.1-A1.4, its inference procedure using the resolution principle can be shown in Figure 2.3.

2.3 Control Strategies for Resolution Method

In Figure 2.3 we can see that some irrelevant and redundant resolvents may be generated in resolution. How to make a decision about which two clauses to be resolved affects efficiency of resolution very much. In order to reduce the number of useless resolvents generated, there have been many control strategies proposed. Here

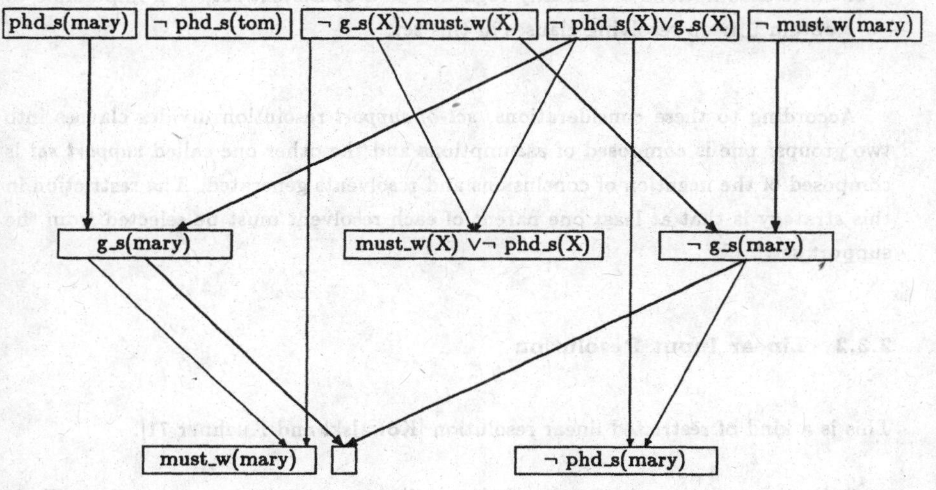

Figure 2.3 An Example of Inference Procedure

we discuss two possible resolution control strategies and evaluate their efficiency and completeness, which will be used to describe the completeness of logic programming in Section 2.4.2.

2.3.1 Set of Support Resolution

This control strategy is based on the following two ideas [Wos et al. 65]:

1. If a set of clauses can be divided into two groups, and clauses in the same group are forbidden to resolve with each other, then the number of clauses generated will be cut down.

2. Since assumptions are usually regarded as a consistent set, it is impossible to obtain □ from resolving clauses in this set.

According to these considerations, ***set-of-support*** resolution divides clauses into two groups: one is composed of assumptions and the other one called ***support set*** is composed of the negation of conclusions and resolvents generated. The restriction in this strategy is that at least one parent of each resolvent must be selected from the support set.

2.3.2 Linear Input Resolution

This is a kind of restricted linear resolution [Kowalski and Kuehner 71].

A ***linear resolution*** is defined as below: all of its resolution paths are kept like a linear structure as shown in Figure 2.4, where C_{i+1} is a resolvent of C_i and B_i, and each B_i is either an input clause (a member of the original set of clauses) or a C_j for some $j, j < i$.

The difference between ***linear resolution*** and ***linear input resolution*** is that B_i (side clause in Figure 2.4) must be an input clause in linear input resolution.

2.3.3 Evaluation of a Control Strategy

There are two important properties of a control strategy: completeness and efficiency. A control strategy of resolution is said to be complete if its use can eventually derive □ whenever inconsistency exists. Even though completeness is important, sometimes it is traded for efficiency. It has been proved that ***set-of-support*** resolution and ***linear*** resolution are complete [Chang and Lee 73], but ***linear input*** resolution is not. Since ***linear input resolution*** only selects the input clauses to resolve it is a very simple and efficient strategy.

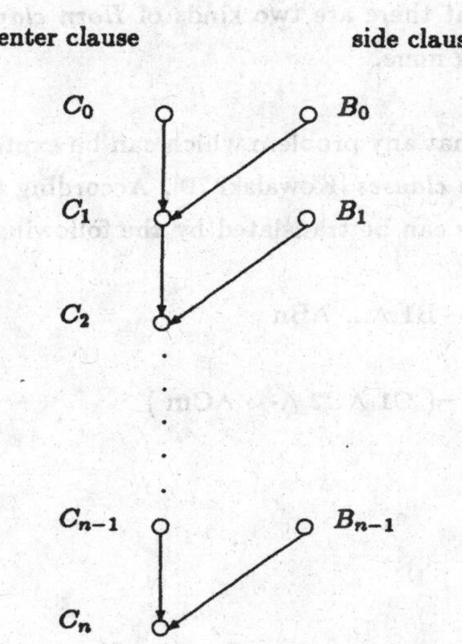

Figure 2.4 Linear Resolution

2.4 Logic Programming

2.4.1 Prolog

Based on various control strategies, many theorem proving systems have been developed. The most successful one, in fact, is not a theorem prover but a logic-based programming language: Prolog. Prolog has become a very famous language and is sometimes regarded as synonymous with logic programming. In Prolog, clauses are restricted to a certain kind of clause called *Horn clause* (actually, extended by negation, disjunctions etc.), so that it can exploit a relatively simple and efficient execution mechanism.

Definition 2.12 A *Horn clause* is a clause which contains at most one positive literal.

Definition 2.12 implies that there are two kinds of *Horn clause* : those with one positive literal and those with none.

It can be shown, in fact, that any problem which can be expressed in logic can be reexpressed by means of *Horn clauses* [Kowalski 79]. According to Definition 2.1 (3), the two kinds of *Horn clauses* can be translated by the following two equivalences:

$$A \vee \neg B1 \vee \cdots \vee \neg Bn = A \leftarrow B1 \wedge \ldots \wedge Bn$$

$$\neg C1 \vee \neg C2 \vee \cdots \vee \neg Cm = \neg(C1 \wedge C2 \wedge \cdots \wedge Cm)$$

The form

$$A \leftarrow B1 \wedge \ldots \wedge Bn$$

is called a *headed clause* , where A and B1 ∧...∧ Bn are called *head* and *body* respectively.

The form

$$\neg(C1 \wedge C2 \wedge, \ldots, \wedge Cm)$$

is called *headless clause.* In Prolog, headed clauses are used to express assumptions, a headless clause is used to express the conclusion. Prolog replaces the symbols "←", "¬" and "∧" by ":-", "?-" and "," respectively. As a result, a Prolog program is a finite set of *Horn clauses* like:

A ←B1 ,B2, ..., Bn.

and a conclusion is like:

?- G1, G2, ..., Gm.

The semantics of a logic program

A ←B1 ,B2, ..., Bn.

can be interpreted in two ways:

(1) declarative : A is implied by B1 and B2 and ... Bn.

(2) procedural : To execute procedure A, call procedure B1, ..., and Bn.

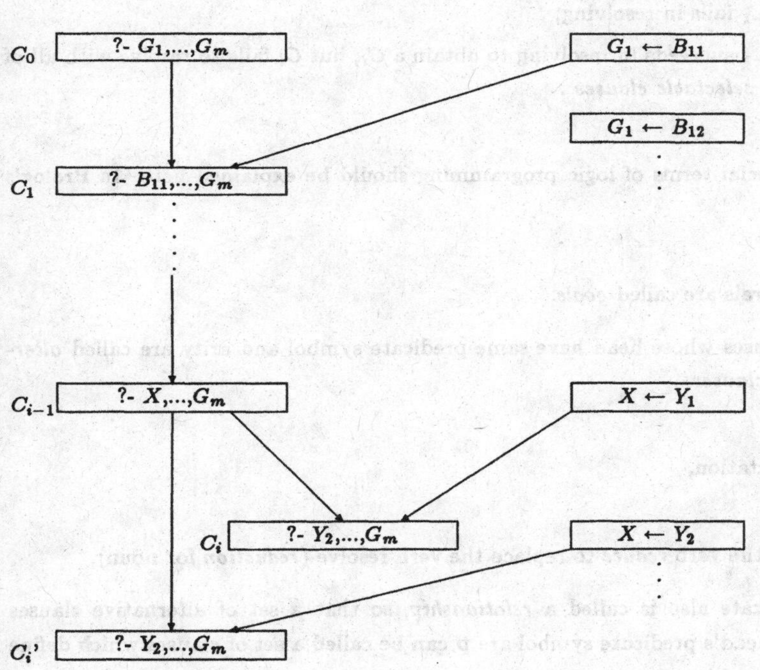

Figure 2.5 The Execution Algorithm of Prolog

The strategy used in Prolog is a restricted linear input strategy named SL (Select Linear input) resolution. The execution algorithm of Prolog is described below

(Figure 2.5):

step 0 it starts at the headless clause, that is

C_0 is ?- G1, ..., Gm.

step i every resolvent C_i is obtained from resolving C_{i-1} and a headed clause whose head is a complement of the first (leftmost) literal of C_{i-1} (we call such a clause C_{i-1}'s *selectable clause*). If there is more than one *selectable clause*, the first one (in sequence of listing) is selected. The rest will be used in order, when the following two cases occur:

1. C_{i-1} fails in resolving;
2. C_{i-1} succeeds in resolving to obtain a C_i, but C_i fails to resolve with all of its *selectable clauses* .

Some special terms of logic programming should be explained here. In Prolog's terminology,

- the literals are called *goals*,
- the clauses whose head have same predicate symbol and arity are called *alternative clauses.*

In this dissertation,

- we use the verb *reduce* to replace the verb resolve (*reduction* for noun),
- a predicate also is called a *relationship*, so that a set of alternative clauses whose head's predicate symbol are p can be called a set of clauses which define a *relationship* p.

If each goal is treated as a node, and unification and reduction are indicated by a dotted line and a solid line respectively, a reduction procedure can be represented as an and-or tree (Figure 2.6). The nodes like H1, H2 and H3 are called or-nodes,

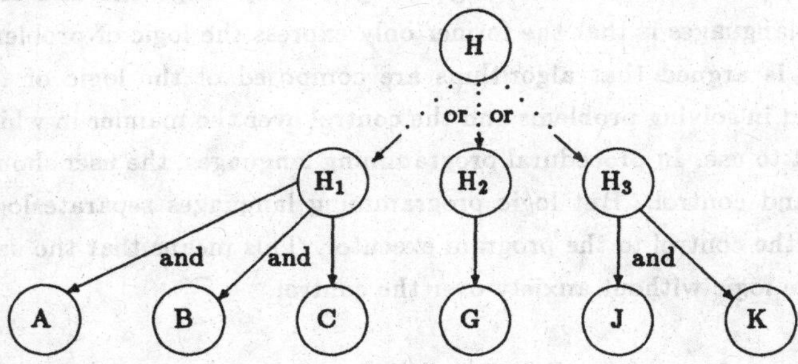

?- H.
$H_1 \leftarrow$ A,B,C.
$H_2 \leftarrow$ G.
$H_3 \leftarrow$ J,K.

Figure 2.6 And-or Tree

and the nodes like A, B, C are called and-nodes. Because in Prolog the leftmost and-node and leftmost or-node are always tried first in every step, the control strategy of Prolog is also called *depth first* search.

Besides *depth first* search, There are also some other kinds of strategies such as *breadth first*, *bounded depth first* and so on. The *breadth first* search means that we always select the nodes in the and-or tree from left to right. The *bounded depth first* search is a mixture of both *depth first* and *breadth first*. That is to say, to some depth of tree, *depth first* is used, and *breadth first* is used temporarily at some depth of the tree.

Next, the advantages and characteristics of logic programming languages are discussed.

The most important difference between logic programming languages and conventional procedural languages is that the former only express the logic of problem-solving methods. It is argued that algorithms are composed of the logic of the information to be used in solving problems and the control over the manner in which the information is put to use. In procedural programming languages, the user should describe both logic and control. But logic programming languages separate logic from control, leaving the control to the program executor. This means that the user need only consider the logic without anxiety over the control.

There are two forms of *non-determinism* in logic programming systems, which were pointed out by [Kowalski 79]:

$non - determinism_1$: when several alternative clauses can unify with a given goal, which clause is selected to try is not determined.

$non - determinism_2$: when several goals in a conjunction need to be executed, the order of execution is not determined.

These two kinds of *non-determinism* are important characteristics of logic programming languages.

2.4.2 The Necessity of Parallel Logic Programming

Prolog's execution algorithm described above is a sequential computation model of logic programming. As a matter of fact, there are at least two kinds of parallelism in a logic program: *and*-parallelism - selecting several goals (not only the leftmost goal) concurrently to reduce; *or*-parallelism - unifying a goal with several clauses (not only the first clause) at the same time. Therefore, as well as the sequential logic programming system Prolog, another research field, parallel logic programming systems, are being studied.

Why is it necessary to make a logic program execute in parallel? The following two main reasons can be considered:

(1) to obtain efficiency

This is the most important reason. In general, it is considered that, in the best case, using *n* processors to process *n* tasks can get *n* times speed up. For logic programming, the merit of parallel (or concurrent) processing, is not only for this reason but also that to process some goals in parallel (concurrently) can avoid much useless searching. For example, if a sorting program is written in the following form:

sort(X,Y) :- permutation(X,Y), order(Y).

This is read as: "list Y is a sorted list from X iff Y is a permutation of X and Y is ordered". If this program is executed by SL resolution, a lot of useless computation in getting the permutation of X will occur. But if the goals permutation(X,Y) and order(Y) are executed in parallel or concurrently, a failure of order(Y) can prevent useless computation of permutation(X,Y) as soon as possible.

(2) to obtain completeness

The SL resolution is not complete since there is a danger of infinite loop in this kind of scheduling. For example, if *integer* is defined like

(1) integer(s(X)) :- integer(X).

(2) integer(0).

Then a goal ?- integer(X) will recurrently unify with Clause (1) forever; for this reason we must put Clause (2) before Clause (1). It means that the sequence of logic program in SL resolution is important. If we execute a logic program in *or* -parallel, the control strategy will be changed. It is no longer SL resolution because it has been freed from the restriction of depth first search. As a result, the strategy turns back to a linear input resolution.

Here, we can prove that a linear input resolution for *Horn clause* is equivalent to a set-of-support resolution.

proof: ($\Rightarrow$) For any resolvent generated by linear input resolution, its one parent belongs to the support set. Therefore we can say that any resolvent generated by

linear input resolution can also be generated by set-of-support resolution.

(⇐) For any resolvent generated by set-of-support resolution,

(1) its pair of parents both belong to the support set, or

(2) one belongs to the support set; another is an input clause.

If set-of-support resolution is applied to a set of *Horn clauses*, case (1) will never occur, since all of the clauses in the support set only have negative literals. Therefore we can say that any resolvent generated by set-of-support resolution can also be generated by linear input resolution.

Q.E.D.

Chapter 3

A Survey of Parallel Logic Languages

This chapter is a survey of parallel logic programming languages.

First, the forms of parallelism in logic programming are classified and defined in detail.

and-parallelism: When there exists more than one goal to be proved, they can be processed in parallel.

or-parallelism: When there exists more than one clauses defined for a relationship, they can be selected for reduction in parallel.

In addition to the above general definitions, *and-parallelism* and *or-parallelism* can be classified more finely.

For *and-parallelism*, there are two kinds of special parallelism included:

restricted and-parallelism: When there exist several goals which have no variable to be shared with each other, they can be processed in parallel.

stream and-parallelism: This is analogous to the stream parallelism of functional programming. That is, two processes which communicate by a sequence of data items can be executed concurrently, where one process is *producer* and the other one is *consumer*.

In the following chapters, the word *and-parallelism* only refers to the two special forms of *and-parallelism* described above, and the term *full and-parallelism* is used for general, unrestricted, *and-parallelism*.

The $non-determinism_1$ is further divided into *don't care non-determinism* and *don't know non-determinism* in [Kowalski 79]. The former refers to the case in which some alternative clauses are not tried after some solution is found. The latter refers to the case in which all the alternative clauses must be tried. *Or-parallelism* can be divided into two different kinds according to Kowalski's classification of $non-determinism_1$.

1. Corresponding to *don't care non-determinism*, there is a kind of *or-parallelism* which can be roughly regarded as or-parallel evaluation of head unification or-parallelism. After this, the evaluation commits to the clause.
2. Corresponding to *don't know non-determinism*, there is the other kind of *or-parallelism* which not only executes head unification in parallel, but also executes all the alternative clauses in parallel to obtain all the solutions.

There have been many approaches to the field of parallel logic programming languages. The approaches are usually classified according to their different computation models and implementation methods. This chapter is not constructed in this way. The approaches to logic programming languages are reviewed here from the viewpoint of design policies. The discussion in this chapter will center on language, namely the user's view of the system. Some surveys of implementation will be distributed between Chapters 5,6,7.

Since this chapter only gives a brief outline of this field, please refer to [Syre and Westphal 85] [Gregory 86] for a detailed review if necessary.

3.1 Completeness versus Efficiency

Section 2.4.2 mentioned some motives for studying parallel logic programming, that is for obtaining efficiency and completeness. But, as a matter of fact, efficiency conflicts with completeness generally. Therefore, there are two kinds of different policies:

1. sacrificing completeness for efficiency;
2. sacrificing some efficiency for completeness.

3.1.1 Completeness

A logic programming system is complete only if the *don't know non-determinism*$_1$ can be really guaranteed.

A complete logic programming system was proposed by Pollard [Pollard 81]. It is designed for a completely unrestrained *full-and*-parallel and *or*-parallel execution of any pure Horn clause program. Pollard's scheme can be described briefly in this way:

- Its and-or tree is constructed in parallel (or by a breadth first scheduler if it is implemented on a single processor machine).
- When a variable shared by more than one goal is bound to multiple solutions from different or-branches, a consistency check (or compatibility check) occurs. The nodes which are not compatible will be canceled from the tree.

Even though this kind of scheme can guarantee completeness, the overhead of its consistency check is too expensive to implement efficiently.

There have also been some complete systems which only consider or-parallelism but not and-parallelism [Tanaka 86] [Ciepielewski 84] [Kasif *et al.* 83] [Lindstrom 84]. One of the problems of or-parallel systems is how to prevent an explosion of search space, and how to execute efficiently.

In fact, for the sake of efficiency, the designers usually do not preserve completeness. Most practical systems to have been developed are incomplete. According to the definition of completeness, an inference system is either complete or incomplete. It seems that to evaluate the completeness, we have no alternative but to answer yes or no. Still, as a matter of fact, we believe that we can give a rough evaluation method for incomplete systems. Here, a comparison method for incompleteness is as follows:

Suppose there is a set of bench mark programs. For two incomplete systems A and B, we say A is more incomplete than B if the number of unsolvable programs in A is more than B.

Using the comparison method above, the incomplete systems can be evaluated more minutely in respect of completeness. Because Prolog has become a very common, useful and efficient system, it can be regarded as a standard. The following system are at least as complete as Prolog.

IC-Prolog, the earliest parallel language developed by Clark *et al.* is a system featuring pseudo and-parallelism [Clark and McCabe 79] [Clark *et al.* 82]. Instead of or-parallelism, IC-Prolog used a global backtracking scheme. This means that the control strategy may be parallel for and-nodes, but is sequential for or-nodes. Like IC-Prolog, Delta-Prolog, another parallel logic programming language features and-parallelism, together with a distributed backtracking scheme [Pereira and Nasr 84]. Both IC-Prolog and Delta-Prolog implement stream and-parallelism. There are also some systems developed to execute restricted and-parallelism [Conery 83] [DeGroot 84]. As mentioned in Section 2.4.1, the strategy used in Prolog is *depth first* search. Clearly, even these inference systems which feature only and-parallelism and backtracking are incomplete, but do not lose 'completeness' compared with Prolog.

A parallel implementation of the Warren abstract machine [Warren 83] is developed by Butler *et al.* [Butler *et al.* 86]. In this abstract machine, goals can be evaluated in either *and*-parallel or *or*-parallel. That is to say, *and-parallelism* and *or-parallelism* can be specified by annotations in a logic program. Although both *and-parallelism* and *or-parallelism* are supported they can not be combined in this proposal: if there is and-parallelism, only one solution can be computed.

The approaches above have a common characteristic: their design policy is to draw out some parallelism for getting efficiency and are at least as complete as Prolog.

3.1.2 Efficiency

On the other side, there are some approaches based on a different policy. They regard the efficiency as the most important, and do not hesitate to sacrifice the form of $non - determinism_1$ named don't know non-determinism, described above.

To allow parallel implementation, Clark et al. gave up IC-Prolog and turned to another way. Absorbing an idea of guarded commands [Dijkstra 75] used in CSP [Hoare 78], Clark and Gregory proposed the Relational Language which incorporated don't care non-determinism, not don't know non-determinism [Clark and Gregory 81]. The Relational Language is based on a special kind of Horn clause called guarded Horn clause which is defined below.

Definition 3.1 A *guarded Horn clause* takes the form

$$A \leftarrow G_1, ..., G_m : B_1, ..., B_n. (m, n \geq 0)$$

here, ':' is called the *commit operator*. It is the same as ',', namely *and* operator, in logic. But it has two special meanings for control:

1. sequential 'and' operator
   Goals after ':' (called the *body*) can not be reduced until all of the goals before ':' (called the *guard*) have succeeded.
2. committed choice
   If a clause successfully reduces the goals in its guard it *commits*, and the execution of the other alternative clauses will be stopped.

According to the above definition, a parallel logic programming system based on guarded Horn clauses is controlled by the following strategies.

1. For *and*-parallelism

All goals inside the guard and the body are resolved in parallel respectively, and the guard part is executed sequentially before the body part.

2. For *or*-parallelism
   Only the guards of alternative clauses are executed in parallel, and if one of them can commit, all of the other alternative clauses will be discarded.

The reason for introducing guarded Horn clauses is to avoid the combination of non-determinism and incremental communication between goals.

Guarded Horn clauses seem to have been becoming the main trend in parallel logic programming languages, especially in Japan. For example, the representative parallel logic programming languages such as Concurrent Prolog [Shapiro 83], PARLOG [Clark and Gregory 83] [Clark and Gregory 86] and GHC [Ueda 85], which have been developed, are all based on guarded Horn clauses. This kind of language is also named 'committed choice non-deterministic languages'.

3.2 Logicality versus Efficiency

A new word *logicality* introduced here should be explained first. When we say a logic language L1 has higher logicality than another logic language L2, it means that the extralogic restrictions in L2 are more than in L1.

As mentioned at the end of Section 2.4.1, since logic programming languages separate logic from control, the user can only consider the logic without anxiety over the control. But it is very difficult to design a control strategy that can work efficiently in most cases. Therefore most practical systems introduce some method of specifying the control. For instance, the 'cut' operator was developed for informing the system where backtracking is unnecessary in Prolog, and for some parallel logic programming system, 'parallel and' and 'sequential and' operators were introduced for telling the system where goals can be executed in parallel [Clark and Gregory 81]. Clearly, the syntactic constructs above do not necessarily restrict logic. On the other hand, some kinds of syntactic constructs have been developed which can improve efficiency but bring some extralogic restrictions too.

Therefore we can say logicality and efficiency are also contradictory to each other in some sense. One should choose, giving consideration to both or emphasizing one of them, before designing.

Until now, a problem related to the above decision is how to build a synchronization mechanism into parallel logic programming languages. This is because the synchronization mechanism may impose some restrictions such that logicality is lost somewhat but efficiency is obtained.

In and-parallel execution, a variable shared by more than one goal plays the role of communication between the goals. It may be more efficient if the system can know which goal is a producer and which goals are consumers. This is the so-called synchronization problem.

Three different synchronization mechanisms are developed in Concurrent Prolog, PARLOG and GHC respectively. In Concurrent Prolog, variable symbols can be suffixed by a mark '?'. This kind of variable (such as X?) is called a *read-only* variable which can be unified with a non-variable term only when X has been bound to a non-variable term. By using *read-only* annotations, system can recognize which variable is an 'input port', and suspend its unification until it has been bound by the other goals. In PARLOG, a *mode* declaration for the clauses is used to state whether each argument of call has input mode or output mode. When the system selects a goal to resolve, it first checks the goal's arguments. If there is an attempt to bind an input mode argument which is an unbound variable the goal will be suspended. In GHC, an explicit syntactic construct is not introduced, but an implicit communication constraint is used. When a goal A is unified with a *guarded Horn clause* A:- G:B, GHC does not allow a unbound variable in the goal side to be bound while resolving the guard G. As a result, an argument which has output mode in PARLOG should be represented as a variable at the head of a clause, and unified after the *commit operator* in GHC.

In contrast, some approaches do not go the way above; they do not like to sacrifice so much logicality. The research described in [Conery 83] [DeGroot 84] is towards a non-annotated program. Conery describes a sophisticated algorithm which is used to analyze dependency of variables dynamically at run-time. According to the dependency, the order of execution of goals is determined. DeGroot improves Conery's

algorithm. He presents a method of compiling Prolog clauses into execution graphs in order to reduce the complexity of analysis of programs.

Chapter 4

P-Prolog: a Parallel Logic Programming Language

In this chapter, a parallel logic language named P-Prolog is presented [Yang and Aiso 86].

The aim of designing P-Prolog is to get as high an efficiency as possible but with a minimum loss of completeness and logicality. When the design of P-Prolog was started, the following problems were taken into consideration.

1.a Though committed choice non-deterministic languages can be implemented very efficiently, they are too incomplete to give a simple logical interface to the user because they do not incorporate *don't know non-determinism.*

1.b On the other hand, it is likely that combining *and*-parallelism and don't know non-determinism for a pure Horn clause program is very difficult.

2.a Annotated synchronization mechanisms result in the pattern of input/output (I/O for short) being fixed when the user writes a program. But, in fact, the ability to execute the same procedure with various I/O patterns is an important feature of a logic language.

2.b On the other hand, the method of compile-time analysis [DeGroot 84] has a weak point: that it can not draw out enough parallelism.

In order to overcome the above problems, P-Prolog, an alternative proposal, was born. It absorbs the advances of guarded Horn clauses while retaining *don't know non-determinism* where required. A novel concept named *exclusive relation of guarded Horn clauses* is introduced in P-Prolog.

The exclusive relation is described in Section 4.1, the syntax and semantics of P-Prolog are presented in Section 4.2. The characteristics of P-Prolog are discussed and compared with other languages by programming examples in Section 4.3. The final two sections of this chapter discuss some theoretic problems relating to P-Prolog.

4.1 Basic Concepts of P-Prolog

4.1.1 Exclusive Guarded Horn Clauses – Synchronization Mechanism

First, we present a definition of the exclusive relation:

Definition 4.1: Exclusive relation.

Exclusive relation EXC($F_1, \ldots, F_n$) is an *n*-ary relation ($n \geq 2$) between truth values of atomic formulas.

$$\begin{aligned} \text{EXC}(F_1, F_2, \ldots, F_n) =_{def} \; & (F_1 \wedge \neg F_2 \ldots \wedge \neg F_n) \vee \\ & (\neg F_1 \wedge F_2 \ldots \wedge \neg F_n) \vee \\ & \ldots \\ & (\neg F_1 \wedge \neg F_2 \ldots \wedge F_n) \end{aligned}$$

namely, if any F_i is true, the others must be false.

When $n = 2$, it is the same as the conventional definition of exclusive-or relation, that is

$$\text{EXC}(F_1, F_2) =_{def} (F_1 \wedge \neg F_2) \vee (\neg F_1 \wedge F_2).$$

Definition 4.2 Committable clause.

When a guarded Horn clause succeeds in unifying with a goal P and successfully executes its guard, we say this clause is *committable* for P.

Definition 4.3: Exclusive Clauses

1. Let C_1, ..., and C_n be alternative guarded Horn clauses:
   (C1). $H_1 \leftarrow G_1 : B_1$.
   ...
   (Cn). $H_n \leftarrow G_n : B_n$.
2. Let **unifiable***(H,P)* stand for whether H can be unified with P. For a goal P, clause C_1, ..., and clause C_n are exclusive if and only if

   EXC(**unifiable**(H_1,P) $\wedge(G_1)s_1$, ... , **unifiable**(H_n ,P) $\wedge(G_n)s_n$)
   Here, s_i is the most general unifier of P with H_i ($i = 1,2, \ldots n$).

We can explain Definition 4.3 simply as follows: a set of alternative guarded Horn clauses is exclusive for a goal P, if and only if there is only one committable clause for P. Clearly, the concept of exclusive clauses is a run-time concept.

The exclusive relation of guarded Horn clauses defined above is used as a synchronization mechanism in P-Prolog. Suppose that of a set of clauses

P $\leftarrow G_1 : B_1$.
P $\leftarrow G_2 : B_2$.
P $\leftarrow G_3 : B_3$.

it is pointed out that these clauses should be exclusive in reducing. When a program executor tries to reduce the goal P, it will check whether the clauses are exclusive for goal P first. If only one clause is committable, it can be reduced. The other case, in which there is more than one committable clause, is not consistent with the exclusive relation. It means that reducing the goal P is not profitable at this time. Therefore the program executor suspends goal P and waits for data input.

For example, a program for summing the elements of a stream is defined as follows:

Program 4.1 summing the elements of a stream

```
(0). summing( S,Total ) : - sum( S,0,Total ).
```

(1). sum([X|Xs],N,Total): – N1 is N + X, sum(Xs,N1,Total).
(2). sum([ ], N, N).

If the user tells the system that clauses (1) and (2) should be exclusive, then a goal **sum**(S,N,T) will be reduced provided that S has been bound to a list. If S is an unbound variable, **sum**(S,N,T) will be suspended, because both (1) and (2) are committable for it in this case.

4.1.2 Non-exclusive Guarded Horn Clauses – Or-parallel Mechanism

Along with the exclusive relation of guarded Horn clauses, we also use a non-exclusive relation in P-Prolog. That is, we can specify that a set of alternative guarded Horn clauses is not exclusive for a goal P.

Non-exclusive clauses are used for don't know non-determinism and or-parallelism. As mentioned in Section 3.1, in the conventional guarded Horn clause, after one clause has committed, the other alternative clauses are discarded. But, in P-Prolog, if some alternative clauses are treated as non-exclusive relation clauses, after one clause C commits, the other ones (if they exist) that are not exclusive to C are not discarded. They will be evaluated in parallel in order to search for all the solutions.

4.2 Syntax and Semantics

4.2.1 Syntax

A P-Prolog program is composed of sets of exclusive and non-exclusive guarded Horn clauses described above. Since this kind of clause has lost the original meaning of guarded command in some sense, we give it a new name, *classified Horn clause.* A classified Horn clauses is formed like:

$$H \leftarrow G_1, ..., G_m : B_1, ..., B_n \quad (m \geq 0, n \geq 0).$$

where H is the head of the clause, the G_i are the guards of the clause, B_i are the bodies of the clause, and ':' is the commit operator. It is read as

H is implied by $G_1, \ldots,$ and G_m and $B_1, \ldots,$ and B_n.

When $m = 0$, it can be expressed as

$$H \leftarrow B_1, \ldots, B_n \qquad (n \geq 0).$$

and it is interpreted as

$$H \leftarrow \text{true} : B_1, \ldots, B_n \qquad (n \geq 0).$$

When $m = 0$ and $n = 0$, it can be expressed as

$H.$ (called unit clause)

and it is interpreted as

$H \leftarrow$ true : true.

As for the '←' operator, it is expressed in the following way:

': –', ': – –', ': – – –', etc

4.2.2 Semantics

As mentioned in Section 4.1, the exclusive relation is introduced into P-Prolog. Some sets of clauses are checked as to whether they are exclusive for the purpose of synchronization. On the other hand, some sets of clauses which are used to search for multiple solutions in parallel need not be checked. For this reason, the system needs information about which groups of clauses should be checked, namely, *expected exclusive clauses.* Therefore, a set of alternative clauses is divided into several subsets in P-Prolog for expressing the exclusive relation between clauses. The semantics of divided subsets is as follows:

1. Clauses in different subsets should be exclusive for a goal P, when they are called by P. This means these clauses must be checked as to whether they are exclusive for P.

2. Clauses in the same subset need not satisfy the exclusive relation when they are called.

In order to express the divided subsets, the implication operator '←' is extended to ': −−', ': − − −' and so on. Though all of ': −', ': −−', ': − − −', etc. read as implying, they have different semantics as follows:

1. A subset in which there is only one clause is indicated by ': −'.

2. A subset having more than one clause is indicated by ': −−', ': − − −' , etc.

For instance, if a relationship is defined by the set of clauses

$$
\begin{array}{l}
H_1 : -G_1 : B_1. \\
H_2 : -G_2 : B_2. \\
H_3 : --G_3 : B_3. \\
H_4 : --G_4 : B_4. \\
H_5 : ---G_5 : B_5. \\
H_6 : ---G_6 : B_6. \\
H_7.
\end{array}
$$

it will be treated as though divided into

$$
\begin{array}{l}
\{H_1 : -G_1 : B_1.\} \\
\{H_2 : -G_2 : B_2.\} \\
\{H_3 : --G_3 : B_3. \quad H_4 : --G_4 : B_4.\} \\
\{H_5 : ---G_5 : B_5. \quad H_6 : ---G_6 : B_6.\} \\
\{H_7\}.
\end{array}
$$

In this case, the two pairs of clauses, H_3 and H_4, H_5 and H_6, are not checked for exclusive relation.

In the current implementation of P-Prolog, we only use ': –'(single neck) and ': ––'(double neck) for simplification, because it seems sufficient for defining a relationship (this is easily extended if necessary). Let us call a clause with ': –' a *single neck clause*, and a *double neck clause* with ': ––'. Then we can give a brief explanation of the exclusive check: An exclusive check does not occur between *double neck clauses.* A check does occur between *single neck clauses*, and also occurs between a *single neck clause* and a *double neck clause.*

We will call the any two clauses between which an exclusive check occurs *expected exclusive clauses.*

In summary, there are three kinds of results in trying to reduce a goal:

(1) **FALSE:** when none of its alternative clauses are committable.

(2) **SUSPEND:** when there exists at least one pair of *expected exclusive clauses* which are both committable.

(3) **REDUCE:** when all pairs of *expected exclusive clauses* are really exclusive, i.e. only one clause of the pair is committable.

4.2.3 Parallelism in Execution

P-Prolog has been developed to feature both *and*- and *or*- parallelism.

For *and*- parallelism,

the goals in the guard and body are evaluated in parallel, and the guard part and body part are evaluated sequentially.

For *or*- parallelism,

1. the alternative clauses are tested in parallel for the committable property (i.e. evaluate head unification and guard), and
2. a set of alternative clauses which are not expected exclusive can be reduced in parallel to search for multiple solutions.

4.2.4 Built-in Predicates

P-Prolog supports a set of built-in predicates similar to conventional sequential logic programming languages. Some differences are explained below.

(1). Built-in Predicates with a Return Value 'suspend'

In a sequential Prolog system, the predicates such as "is", ">", etc. return an answer *false* or *error* when their arguments are unbound. In P-Prolog, an answer *suspend* will be returned in this case. We also support some built-in predicates which are suspended for variables. For example, we introduced '@write' and '@==' which are the same as 'write' and '==' when their arguments are non-variable terms. But, when their arguments are unbound, the former will be suspended while the latter will be executed.

(2). Special Operator - 'other'

In P-Prolog, the reduction can be controlled by the built-in predicate *'other'*, which must appear in a guard. It is used to separate the single neck clauses into several groups. For example,

$$H_1 : -G_1 : B_1.$$
$$H_2 : -G_2 : B_2.$$
$$H_3 : -other, G_3 : B_3.$$
$$H_4 : -G_4 : B_4.$$

is divided into two groups: $\{ H_1, H_2 \}$ and $\{ H_3, H_4 \}$.

The relation between the separated groups is a committed choice. This means that if one group can be reduced then the subsequent groups will not be tried, or their execution will be terminated.

As mentioned above, 'other' is used to separate the single neck clauses into several groups. therefore, we can also use the other kind of syntax construct instead of 'other'

operator, such as bracket, semicolon and so on.

(3). seq

Because there are some problems which must be evaluated sequentially, a built-in predicate seq(X) is supported(X is a series of goals). seq(X) will evaluate X with a depth first scheduler.

(4). setof

In conventional sequential programming logic languages and PARLOG, a built-in predicate:

setof(List,Goal,Var)

is defined, to collect all the solutions of Goal's Var into List. P-Prolog also supports it. It can also be used in a form:

setof(List,Var).

This allows us to write

(1) ..., Goal, setof(List,Var) ,...

instead of

(2) setof(List,Goal,Var).

The difference between them is form (1) collects the solutions in both and- and or- parallelism, but form (2) collects the solutions in only or- parallelism.

4.3 Programming Example and Comparison with Other Languages

This section compares the capabilities of P-Prolog with three representative parallel logic programming languages - Concurrent Prolog, PARLOG and GHC - by programming examples. All of the examples in this paper have been tested using a prototype interpreter of P-Prolog.

4.3.1 Simplicity

An efficient sort algorithm [Hoare 61] can be expressed in P-Prolog as follows.

Program 4.2 quick sort

```
(1) quicksort( Unsorted,Sorted ): -
            qsort( Unsorted,Sorted,[ ] ).

(2) qsort( [X|Unsorted], Sorted, Rest ): -
            partition( Unsorted,X,Smaller,Larger ),
            qsort( Smaller,Sorted,[X|Sorted1]),
            qsort(Larger,Sorted1,Rest).
(3) qsort( [ ],Rest,Rest ).

(4) partition([X|Xs],A,Smaller,[X|Larger]): -
            A < X : partition(Xs,A,Smaller,Larger).
(5) partition([X|Xs],A,[X|Smaller],Larger): -
            A >= X : partition(Xs,A,Smaller,Larger).
(6) partition([ ],_,[ ],[ ]).
```

Three *quick sort* programs written by the other languages are listed in Figure 4.1, because the direct way for comparing the simplicity is to list a program which describes the same algorithm for each language. Comparing Program 4.2 with the programs in Figure 4.1, it is obvious that P-Prolog is the simplest. In Concurrent Prolog, users must think about which variables are read-only. In PARLOG, users

(the differences with P-Prolog are marked by under line)

** quick sort by Concurrent Prolog*

```
quicksort( Unsorted,Sorted ):-
        qsort( Unsorted,Sorted,[] ).

qsort( [X|Unsorted], Sorted, Rest ):-
        partition( Unsorted?, X,Smaller,Larger ),
        qsort( Smaller?, Sorted,[X|Sorted1] ),
        qsort( Larger?, Sorted1,Rest ).
qsort( [],Rest,Rest ).
```

```
partition([X|Xs],A,Smaller,[X|Larger]):-
        A < X : partition( Xs?, A,Smaller,Larger ).

partition([X|Xs],A,[X|Smaller],Larger):-
        A >= X : partition( Xs?, A,Smaller,Larger).

partition([],_,[],[]).
```

** quick sort by PARLOG*

```
mode quicksort( ?, ^ ).
mode qsort( ?, ^, ^ ).
mode partition( ?, ?, ^, ^ ).

quicksort( Unsorted,Sorted ):-
        qsort( Unsorted,Sorted,[] ).

qsort( [X|Unsorted], Sorted, Rest ):-
        partition( Unsorted,X,Smaller,Larger ),
        qsort( Smaller,Sorted,[X|Sorted1]),
        qsort(Larger,Sorted1,Rest).
qsort( [],Rest,Rest ).
```

```
partition([X|Xs],A,Smaller,[X|Larger]):-
        A < X : partition(Xs,A,Smaller,Larger).

partition([X|Xs],A,[X|Smaller],Larger):-
        A >= X : partition(Xs,A,Smaller,Larger).

partition([],_,[],[]).
```

** quick sort by GHC*

```
quicksort( Unsorted,Sorted ):-
        true : qsort( Unsorted,Sorted,[] ).

qsort( [X|Unsorted], Sorted, Rest ):-
        true :
        partition( Unsorted,X,Smaller,Larger ),
        qsort( Smaller,Sorted,[X|Sorted1]),
        qsort(Larger,Sorted1,Rest).

qsort( [], Rest0,Rest1 ):- true : Rest0 = Rest1.
```

```
partition([X|Xs],A,Smaller, Larger):-
        A < X : Larger=[X|L1],
        partition(Xs,A,Smaller,L1).

partition([X|Xs],A, Smaller, Larger):-
        A >= X : Smaller=[X|L1],
        partition(Xs,A,S1,Larger).

partition([],_, Smaller,Larger):- true :
        Smaller=[], Larger=[].
```

Figure 4.1 Quick Sort Programs in Concurrent Prolog, PARLOG and GHC

must add a mode declaration for every predicate. And in GHC, users must avoid allowing a variable in a goal unify with any instances before the clause to be committed. But, in P-Prolog, except for substituting the commit operator ':' for the cut operator '!', Program 4.2 is exactly the same as a quicksort program written by the sequential logic programming language Prolog. (It may be hard to believe that this program can be executed in parallel.)

A simple example ?- quicksort([2,1,3],X) described below, demonstrates how it works and how processes are synchronized with each other by exclusive relation checking. A flow diagram for the execution is shown in Figure 4.2. To save space, we substitute p and qs for partition and qsort, respectively. At step 0, we have an initial goal quicksort([2,1,3],X). Every step i is the result from the reduction of the goals of step i-1. The numbered arrow(marked by n) between the two blocks A and B means that a unification between A and the n_th clause defined in Program 4.2 produces B. The line arrow indicates a suspension from reducing. For instance, at step 2, p([1,3],2,S,L), qs(S,X,[2|W]) and qs(L,W,[ ]) try to reduce. Obviously, p([1,3],2,S,L) can be reduced to p([3],2,S1,L1) by unifying it with clause 5. But qs(S,X,[2|W]) and qs(L,W,[ ]) are suspended because they successfully unify with two clauses(2 and 3 in Program 4.2) which are *expected exclusive clauses.* After step 3, S is bound to [1|S1], so there is only one clause that is committable. Therefore qs(S,X,[2|W]) can be reduced immediately. Lastly, at step 7 all clauses have been reduced to true, then the execution is stopped and a sorted list [1,2,3] is obtained.

Another example is shown below. Like other parallel logic programming languages, streams are used to communicate between the distributed processes in P-Prolog. To implement stream I/O functions, the two programs named in_stream and out_stream can be defined as follows:

Program 4.3 stream I/O

```
(1) in_stream( [X|Xs] ): – read(X) : in_stream(Xs).

(2) out_stream( [ ] ).
(3) out_stream( [X|Xs] ): – write(X) , out_stream(Xs).
```

Here, read and write are built-in predicates for inputting or outputting a term

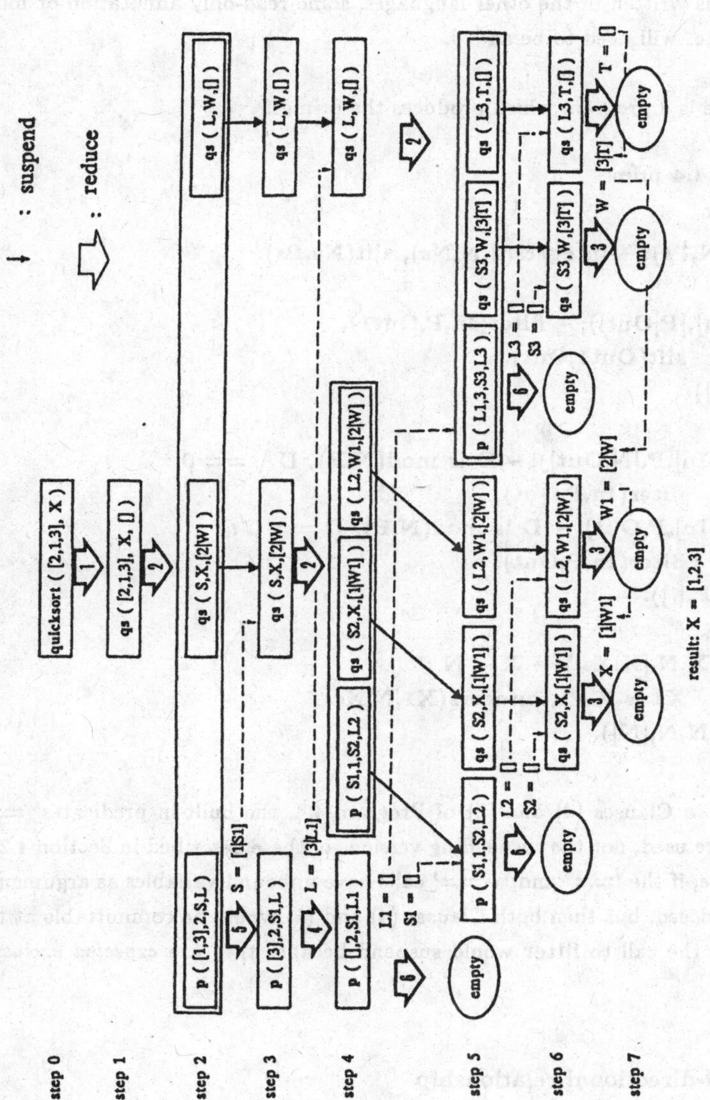

Figure 4.2 The Execution of ?- quicksort([2,1,3],X).

from or to a terminal. The end of the input stream is ignored for simplification. If this program is written in the other languages, some read-only annotation or mode declaration, etc. will need to be added.

Next, there is a program which produces the primes.

Program 4.4 primes

```
(1) primes(N,Ps): - integers(2,N,Ns), sift(Ns,Ps).

(2) sift([P|In],[P|Out]): - filter(In,P,Out1),
                  sift(Out1,Out).
(3) sift([ ],[ ]).

(4) filter([N|In],P,[N|Out]): - D is mod(N,P), D \ == 0 :
                  filter(In,P,Out).
(5) filter([N|In],P,Out): - D is mod(N,P), D == 0 :
                  filter(In,P,Out).
(6) filter([ ],P,[ ]).

(7) integers(X,N,[X|Xs]): - X < N :
                  X1 is X+1, integers(X1,N,Xs).
(8) integers(N,N,[N]).
```

Note that, in Clauses (4) and (5) of Program 4.4, the built-in predicates '==' and '\ ==' are used, not the suspending versions of these described in Section 4.2.4. This is because, if the '==' and '\ ==' calls have unbound variables as arguments, they would succeed, but then both Clauses (4) and (5) would be committable at the same time, so the call to filter would suspend because they are *expected exclusive clauses.*

4.3.2 Multi-directional relationship

The examples described in Program 4.1,4.2,4.3 and 4.4 have a common characteristic, namely, single direction. For this kind of problem P-Prolog has the same capability as the committed choice non-deterministic languages, but gives a simpler interface to the user. Besides this kind of problem there are a lot of other problems in which a multi-directional relationship is described, such as **append, merge** ... and so on. In committed choice non-deterministic logic programming languages, I/O patterns have been fixed for every relationship in such a way that it is difficult to define a multi-directional relationship. But in P-Prolog it is easy to do this.

Program 4.5 merge and strict split

```
(1) merge( [X|Xs],Y,[X|Zs] ): - merge( Y,Xs,Zs ).
(2) merge( [ ],Y,Y ).
(3) merge( X,[Y|Ys],[Y|Zs] ): - other : merge( Ys,X,Zs ).
(4) merge( X,[ ],X ).
```

This program can be executed using several I/O patterns: merge(in, in, out), merge(in, out, in), merge(out, in, in), and merge(in, in, in). Here, 'in' denotes input and 'out' denotes output. Because there is an **other** in the guard of Clause (3), Clause (1) and Clause (2) will be tried for execution before Clause (3) and Clause (4). To merge two input streams **S1** and **S2** to **X**, it works as follows. If the first argument of the call is a substitution instance of a non-empty list, then only Clause (1) can be committed, so Clause (1) will be reduced. If the first argument is an unbound variable, then Clause (1) and Clause (2) are committable at the same time, so that they can not be executed at this moment. Therefore, Clause (3) and Clause (4) will be tried next. Now, if the second argument is also an unbound variable, the call will be suspended and wait for input, otherwise Clause (3) or Clause (4) may be committable depending on the value of the second argument.

Besides this I/O pattern, this program can also be used to accept two input streams **X, S1**, and produce an output stream **S2** which is a split stream created by separating **S1** from **X**. For instance, if the first argument and the third argument are non-empty lists, either Clause (1) or Clause (3) will be committable to candidacy depending on whether or not the first elements of the two lists are the same.

The behavior of Program 4.5 is shown in Figure 4.3. The synchronization mechanism allows a clause to commit only if more than one stream is available at any port

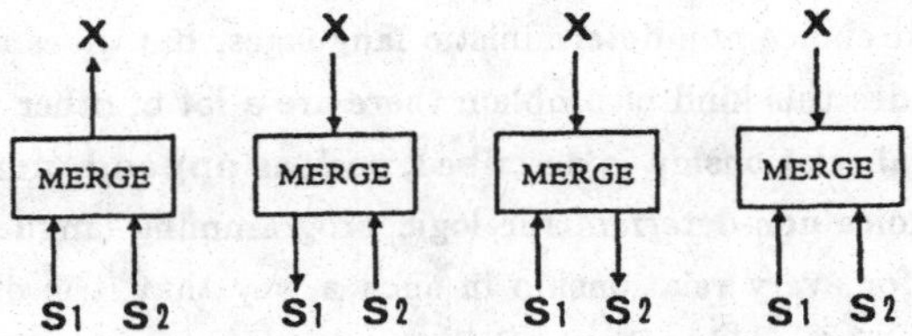

Figure 4.3 Muiti-directional of Merge

(the position of argument), or if one stream is available at the first or the second port.

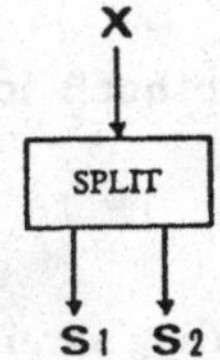

Figure 4.4 A Split

If we want to expand its I/O pattern so that it can accept a stream at the third port, and output two split streams (Figure 4.4), we can rewrite Program 4.5 as follows:

Program 4.6 merge and split

```
(1) merge( [X|Xs],Y,[X|Zs] ): – merge( Y,Xs,Zs ).
(2) merge( [ ],Y,Y ).
(3) merge( X,[Y|Ys],[Y|Zs] ): – other : merge( Ys,X,Zs ).
(4) merge( X,[ ],X ): – var(X) : true.
(5) merge( [ ],[ ],[ ] ).
```

Clause (4) in Program 4.5 is replaced by Clause (4) and Clause (5) in Program 4.6. The reason of adding

```
merge( [ ],[ ],[ ] )
```

is that it is necessary to use different kind of instances at the third port in order to express the exclusive relation relating to the third port.

```
merge( X,[ ],X ): - var(X) : true.
```

is the same as

```
merge( X,[ ],X ).
```

in logic. The purpose of adding var(X) is to keep the exclusive relation between Clause (3) and Clause (4), also Clause (5) and Clause (4) in the case where only the third argument is available.

Another interesting example is rewriting the above sort program so that it can also be regarded as a permutation program.

Program 4.7 sort and permutation

```
(1) qsort( [X|Unsorted], Sorted ): - Sorted \== [ ] :
            partition( Unsorted,X,Smaller,Larger ),
            qsort( Smaller,Sorted1 ),
            qsort(Larger,Sorted2 ),
            append( Sorted1,[X|Sorted2],Sorted ).
(2) qsort( [ ],[ ] ).

(3) partition([X|Xs],A,Smaller,[X|Larger]): --
            A < X : partition(Xs,A,Smaller,Larger).
(4) partition([X|Xs],A,[X|Smaller],Larger): --
            A >= X : partition(Xs,A,Smaller,Larger).
(5) partition([ ],_,[ ],[ ]).
```

(append is defined in Program 4.9)

Program 4.7 can be used to execute a goal such as ?- qsort(X,[1,2,3]), and it will give six solutions of X, namely [1,2,3], [1,3,2], [2,3,1], [2,1,3], [3,1,2] and [3,2,1].

Because P-Prolog uses exclusive relations to synchronize, one relationship can be defined multi-directionally, and the streams can change their directions dynamically.

4.3.3 Not Only *Don't care Non-determinism* but also *Don't know Non-determinism*

In P-Prolog, the clauses defined as *expected exclusive clauses* are evaluated in the conventional way called 'committed choice non-determinism' in which only one clause is reduced, and the others are discarded. Along with *expected exclusive clauses*, we can use the non-exclusive relation to specify or-parallelism for all solution searching. The clauses defined as *expected non-exclusive clauses* (double neck clauses) are executed in parallel. Their commit operator has lost the original meaning of committed choice; it just plays the role of a sequential-and operator. This syntax style (i.e. expected non-exclusive clauses) is very convenient. For instance, a program for finding an element in the intersection of two lists can be written in P-Prolog as follows:

Program 4.8 intersect

```
(1) intersect( X,L1,L2 ): - member( X,L1 ), member( X,L2 ).

(2) member( X,[X|_] ): -- true.
(3) member( X,[_|Y] ): -- member( X,Y ).
```

Because Clauses (2) and (3) are *double neck clauses*, success in committing one of them does not exclude the other. As a result, call **member(X,L)** can be evaluated in parallel, and more than one solution of **X** will be returned from different search paths. If the second argument of **member** is sent from another process dynamically, it is necessary to synchronize it. In this case, the relationship of **member** can be defined as follows:

```
(1) member( X, [X|Y] ): -- Y \== [ ] : true.
(2) member( X, [_|Y] ): -- Y \== [ ] : member( X,Y ).
(3) member( X, [X] ).
```

Compared with P-Prolog, in committed choice non-deterministic languages this kind of program can not work correctly, because if the first member find a value for X, it will be regarded as the single solution even it this choice does not suit the second member.

4.4 Programming in P-Prolog

When a program is written in P-Prolog, the important point is how to decide which clause is *single neck* or *double neck*.

To decide between *single* or *double* neck, we can roughly say:

1. for a set of alternative clauses, if we expect that only one of them is committable, we should write them as single neck clauses,
2. otherwise, if we want to let the alternative clauses be executed in or-parallel, double necks should be used.

To make this more precise, we give two definitions below. First, we give a definition of the relationship's *universe*.

Definition 4.4: Let S be a set of clauses of which our program is composed, and H be a Hebrand universe (see Def 2.2) of S. For any *n*-ary relationship P defined in S, its *universe* U is an infinite set defined as

$$U =_{def} \bigcup_{i=0}^{\infty}(P(x_{i1}, ..., x_{in}))$$

here, $x_{ij} \in$ H or x_{ij} is unbound.

Definition 4.5: Let U be a universe of P in a set S. A *subuniverse* of P named U_s is a subset of U. That is,

$$U_s \subseteq U.$$

When we define a relationship P, a subuniverse U_s of P is usually considered (U_s = U , if not to be considered). Therefore, one of the basic rules may be summarized as: *expected exclusive clauses* (single neck clauses) should be exclusive for U_s.

For example, a program appending two lists can be written as

```
(1) append([ ],X,X).
(2) append([X|Y],Z,[X|W]): - append(Y,Z,W).
```

for a U_s which is composed of all goals whose first argument is a list.

If U_s = U, the **append** program will be rewritten as:

```
(1) append([ ],X,X): -- true.
(2) append([X|Y],Z,[X|W]): -- append(Y,Z,W).
```

If we want to restrict U_s to a special set which does not include the goals all of whose arguments are unbound, the **append** program can be written as follows:

Program 4.9 append

```
append([ ],X,X): -- X \ == [ ] : true.
append([X|Y],Z,[X|W]): -- append(Y,Z,W).
append([ ],[ ],[ ]).
```

There is another **append** whose U_s is composed by all of the goals which at least have two list arguments.

Program 4.10 append

```
(1) append([ ],X,X).
(2) append([X|Y],Z,[X|W]): - Z \ ==[X|W] : append(Y,Z,W).
```

4.5 Re-examination of P-Prolog in Terms of Theory

First, two special cases of P-Prolog are discussed here:

1. a subset of P-Prolog using only *single neck clauses*, and

2. a subset of P-Prolog using only *double neck clauses*.

The former is an and-parallel logic language, and cannot search for multiple solutions in parallel. It is similar to Concurrent Prolog, PARLOG and GHC etc. from this point of view. As for the latter, it can be regarded as a parallel logic language without a synchronization mechanism and guarded command, namely, pure Horn clauses. Therefore, we can regard the clauses in P-Prolog (called classified Horn clauses) as an intermediate form between pure Horn clauses and guarded Horn clauses.

But the significance of classified Horn clauses is not only that. From the viewpoint of inference systems, an important difference between a set of guarded Horn clauses and classified Horn clauses is as follows:

- guarded Horn clauses only support some specifications to affect the control strategy of inference.

- classified Horn clauses not only support specifications for control, but also bring a change into the original logical meaning of clauses.

For example, a set of guarded Horn clauses

{ P1 ←G1 : B1 .
  P2 ←G2 : B2 . }

has the declarative semantics:

P1 is implied by G1 and B1;
P2 is implied by G2 and B2.

But a set of classified Horn clauses:

{ P1 ←G1 : B1 .
P2 ←G2 : B2 . }

has a different declarative semantics:

P1 is implied by G1 and B1;
P2 is implied by G2 and B2.
and if P1 holds P2 should fail,
conversely, if P2 holds P1 should fail.

Therefore, we can say, in terms of theory, compared with the existing logic programming languages, one of the important improvements of P-Prolog is to use logic to express control.

As for synchronization, in contrast to the other parallel logic languages, in P-Prolog, users pay attention to the exclusive relation between clauses rather than the declaration of I/O pattern. It seems to us that P-Prolog has more logicality than the others.

Lastly, completeness of P-Prolog is discussed here. It depends on the scheduling method of practical system. In Section 4.2.3, P-Prolog's parallelism in execution has been noted. If P-Prolog is really implemented in that way (namely ***breadth first*** scheduling or ***bounded depth-first scheduling***), it is a complete system. Otherwise, it is incomplete, but it is 'more complete' than committed choice non-deterministic languages.

Part II

IMPLEMENTATION

Chapter 5

Binary Tree Expression

It is known that the data structure in logic programming languages (generally speaking, in nonnumeric computation) is very different than in numeric computation. In numeric computation regular structured data are taken as the primary objects, but in logic programming non-regular structured data are taken as the primary objects.

As defined in Section 2.1, *term, literal* and *clause*, the primary objects in logic programming languages, are structured like tree whose components may be of different types, and may be defined in a recursive form. This kind of structure is called *tree structured data* here. In this chapter, a general implementation problem, how tree structured data can be processed efficiently, will be discussed [Yang *et al.* 86a] [Yang *et al.* 86a].

5.1 Binary Tree Memory

The tree structured data usually is represented like the form shown in Figure 5.1, when they are stored in a conventional linear addressing memory. In this form, if a component is a compound term, a pointer is used to point to it. Besides this, there is another representation called a LIST representation (Figure 5.2) for representing tree structured data. In the conventional implementation of Prolog systems, tree structured data is usually represented in one or both of these forms. There is a common feature in these two types of representation: pointers must be used. The

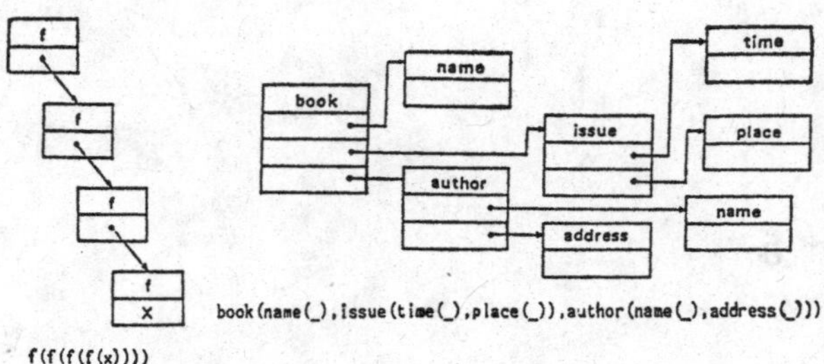

Figure 5.1 Representation of Tree Structured Data (1)

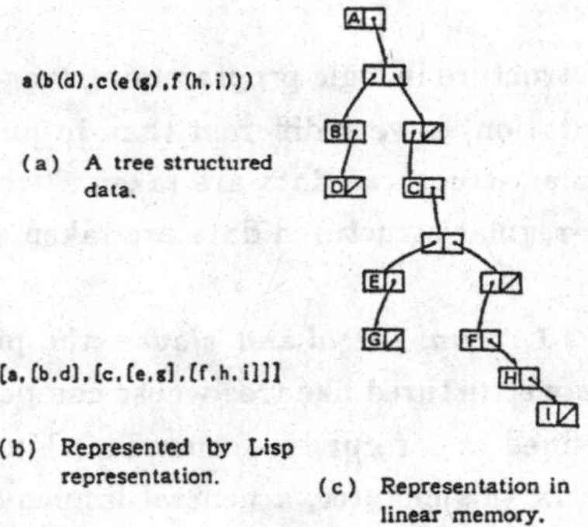

Figure 5.2 Representation of Tree Structured Data (2)

advantage of pointers is their flexibility. We can use them to connect two operands which are loaded at any location. It is necessary to use pointers when we want to process shared structures efficiently. But on the other cases, overhead will be caused by processing pointers. For instance, from Figure 5.1 and Figure 5.2, we can see that about 40% of the data space is occupied by pointers such that nearly half of the accessed time and memory space are wasted for the sake of pointers. If we reduce the overhead of pointer processing, the tree structured data can be processed far more efficiently, and as a result, the total efficiency of a Prolog machine can be improved greatly. For this reason it is essential to develop a special memory model for tree processing. With this idea in mind, a new memory type called BTM is presented below.

The basic point of view is that we must abandon the concept of linear addressing and present a memory model in which the predecessor or successor of any node can be directly accessed. Because a binary tree is a kind of standard tree, it can be processed easier than an arbitrary tree. And any arbitrary tree may be transformed into a binary tree provided that a transformation function is defined. For example, we can suppose that for all nodes in a binary tree they have brother relation with their right node and parent-child relation with their left node (Figure 5.3 (b)). Then the arbitrary tree shown in Figure 5.3 (a) will be transformed into the binary tree shown in Figure 5.3 (c) [Knuth 68]. For these reasons we need only consider binary trees in our research.

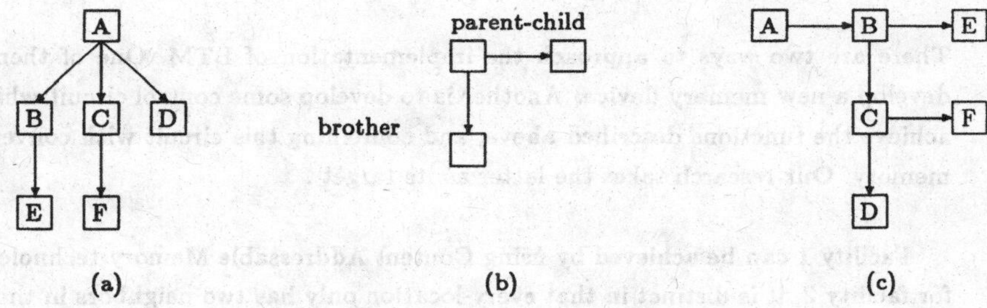

Figure 5.3 Transformation From Arbitrary to Binary Tree

The conceptual image of a BTM is defined as follows:

BTM is used to record the binary trees in which each node stores data (labeled tree). This is different from the LISP binary trees, because in the LISP binary trees, only leaf nodes store data, and all of the other nodes store pointers (unlabeled tree).

The facilities of BTM are

1. The root node can be accessed directly provided that the name of tree is submitted.
2. From any node, the predecessor and successor can be accessed directly without using pointers.

In comparison with other memories, the feature of several different kinds of memories are as follows:

Linear addressing memory **Addressing depending on a cell's address**

Content addressable memory **Addressing depending on a cell's content**

Binary tree memory **Addressing depending on the current node and direction**

5.2 Functions for Computing Node's Address

There are two ways to approach the implementation of BTM. One of them is to develop a new memory device. Another is to develop some control circuit which can achieve the functions described above, and combining this circuit with conventional memory. Our research takes the latter as its target .

Facility 1 can be achieved by using Content Addressable Memory technology. As for facility 2, it is distinct in that every location only has two neighbors in the linear addressing memory, and therefore it is impossible to store the connected nodes of a binary tree in consecutive locations. For this reason the problem to be solved is how we can represent the relation between two nodes which connect each other in logic, but not in physics. A basic method for solving this problem is to define the function

F(node, dir)

Here, the field of the function F is a memory address space, node is the address of memory and dir points out the direction of next access (dir $\in$ {upward,left,right }).

F must satisfy the two following conditions:

1. **node = F(F(node,left), upward) = F(F(node, right), upward)**
2. **Memory space can be utilized economically.**

A binary tree may be loaded into memory by computing the function defined above. In other word if the address of the current node and direction are given, the address of its predecessor or successor can be calculated by this function. As a result, the connection between nodes is not the pointer, but the calculation of a function. Next, several functions are discussed.

(1). Vector Representation (Figure 5.4)

This is a traditional representation method for a complete binary tree [Wulf et al 81]. A complete binary tree refers to a binary tree in which every node has two successors.

$$F(node, dir) = \begin{cases} 2 \times node & \text{dir} = \text{left} \\ 2 \times node + 1 & \text{dir} = \text{right} \\ node/2 & \text{dir} = \text{up} \end{cases} \quad (5.1)$$

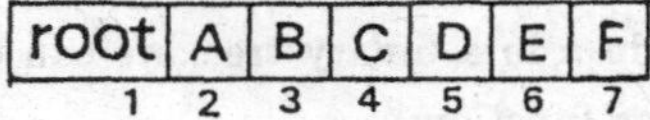

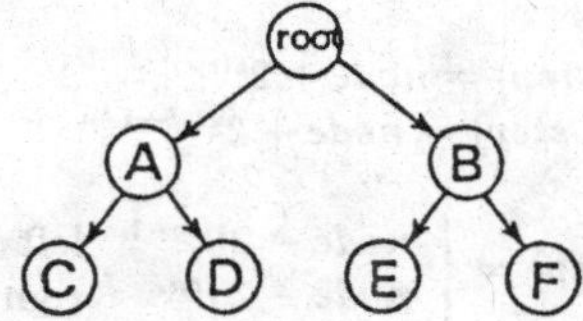

Figure 5.4 A Binary Tree Stored in Vector Function

A function defined in formula (**5.1**) is only suitable for a complete binary tree. A lot of memory space will be wasted when an arbitrary binary tree is represented in this way. To solve this problem, we investigated the following functions.

(2). Breakdown Function

First, a function which is also only suitable for complete trees is introduced. The method of computing the node's address can be explained as follows (Figure 5.5):

Suppose: the root is 0.

step 0 the left-son of 0 is 1 (0+1); the right-son of 0 is 2 (0+2),

step 1 the left-son of 1 is 3 (1+2); the right-son of 1 is 5 (1+4), and the left-son of 2 is 4 (2+2); the right-son of 2 is 6 (2+4),

... ...

step i the left-son of n is $n + 2^i$, the right-son of n is $n + 2^{i+1}$

... ...

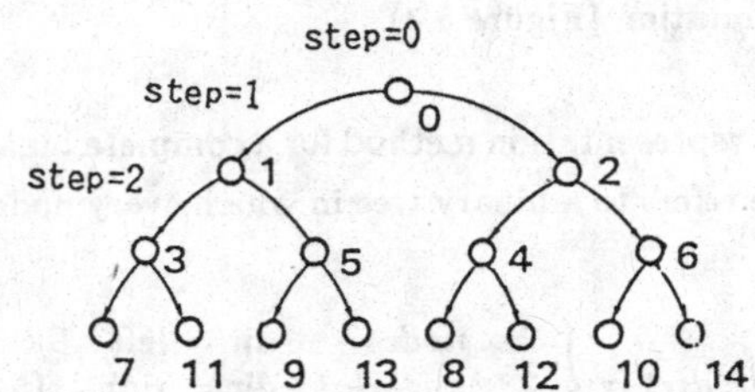

Figure 5.5 A Binary Tree Stored in Breakdown Function

To sum up, for any node n in a binary tree, we can obtain its predecessor and successor using the following function:

$$
\begin{aligned}
&left\_son(node, step) = node + 2^{step} \\
&right\_son(node, step) = node + 2^{step+1} \\
&father(node, step) = \begin{cases} node - 2^{step-1} & \text{left node} \\ node - 2^{step} & \text{right node} \end{cases}
\end{aligned}
\qquad (5.2)
$$

This function has some advantages which will be discussed in the next chapter, though it is only suitable for complete binary trees, like the vector function.

(3). Step Count Function

Based on the breakdown function, an optimized function can be developed to obtain greater memory utilization.

We introduce two auxiliary arguments named **state** and **step**, such that **F** becomes

F(node, dir, state, step)

where **state** is a tag of 4 bits, which identifies the state of the node regarding the number of successors, number of others, etc. The first bit from the left is called the **brother bit**, whose value is set to '0' if the node has no brothers, and '1' otherwise. The second bit is called **position bit** which is used to distinguish the position of a node, '0' means that this node is a left successor and '1' means that it is a right successor. The other two bits are called **son bit** standing for the number of successors (0,1,2). And when a **son bit** is 3, it means that the node is a root. In this special case, the **position bit** and the **brother bit** lose their original meaning, they stand for the number of successors instead of the **son bit**. Another argument named **step** is used to record the history of branch. The initial value of **step** is zero. After branching(in other words, if the node has two successors) **step** will be incremented by one. If the node has one successor, **step** will not be changed.

F(node,dir,state,step) is defined as follows. If the notation ø appears in **state**, it means that we don't care what the value of this bit is. In other words, it means that this bit may be '0' or '1'.

$$\begin{aligned}
&F(node, L, \ \o\o 10, step) = node + 2^{step} \\
&F(node, R, \ \o\o 10, step) = node + 2^{step+1} \\
&F(node, LR, \o\o 01, step) = node + 2^{step} \\
& \\
&F(node, U, \ 0\o\o\o, step) = node - 2^{step} \\
&F(node, U, \ 11\o\o, step) = node - 2^{step} \\
&F(node, U, \ 10\o\o, step) = node - 2^{step-1}
\end{aligned} \qquad (5.3)$$

$$L: left, \quad R: right, \quad LR: left\ or\ right, \quad U: up$$

In Figure 5.6 several examples are shown to illustrate how binary trees are loaded by Formula (5.3).

(4) Distance Function

A weak point of method 2 is that the rate of memory utilization may be cut down if the tree is unbalanced. Therefore another method is introduced here.

$$F(node, dir, dif) = \begin{cases} node + 1 & \text{dir} = \text{left} \\ node + dif & \text{dir} = \text{right} \end{cases} \qquad (5.4)$$

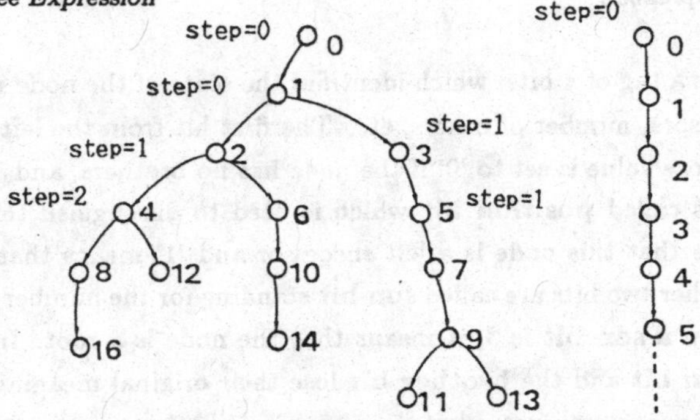

Figure 5.6 A Binary Tree Stored in Step Count Function

Here, dif is equal to the size of a node's subtree increased by one. Figure 5.7 shows an example of a binary tree loaded by formula (5.4).

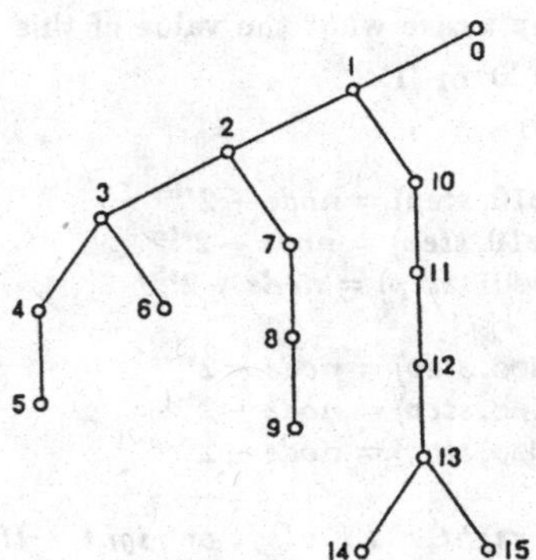

Figure 5.7 A Binary Tree Stored in Distance Function

If we compare the four functions, the problem of *vector function* and *breakdown function* is that when an arbitrary binary tree is loaded into memory in this way, a lot of empty cells may appear inside the tree's area causing the rate of memory utilization to be cut down. In comparison with *vector* and *breakdown functions*, *step count* function improves the rate of memory utilization considerably, because branch information is stored in every node, and depending on this information the calculating method may be changed for the sake of reducing empty cells. Function 2 is suitable for dynamic balanced binary trees. In comparison the others *distance function* has the advantage that no empty cell appear in the tree's area. Therefore there is no problem in the rate of memory utilization. But in this way it can only process static trees which have a determinate structure, and the predecessor can not be accessed from the right successor in *distance function*.

There is a contradiction when we take conventional memory as a base, and add special hardware for calculating addresses. That is, it is difficult to satisfy requirements for the flexibility of data structure and the rate of memory utilization at the same time. But we can choose a different method for different requirements. For instance, in a Prolog system data which appears in the program area is static, and the execution environment has dynamic data. We can select a different method for each of them.

5.3 Data Expression by Binary Tree

This section discusses how to express tree structured data of logic languages by the binary tree.

(1) Expressions of terms

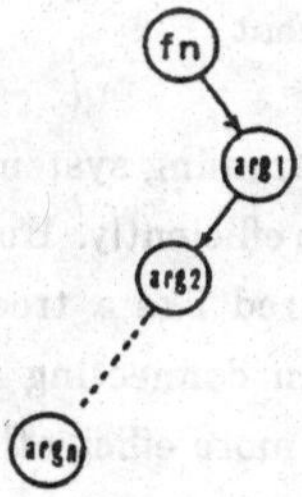

Figure 5.8 BTM Expressions of fn(arg1,arg2,...,argN)

A term such as **fn(arg1,arg2,...,argN)** is expressed like the format shown in Figure 5.8. If each argument is also structured data, the same format is used to express such an argument. For example, we use the binary tree shown in Figure 5.9(a) to express **fn(fn1(X1,X2),fn2(X2,Y2),Z)**. In order to increase the efficiency, for the expression of list structures, we use the format shown in Figure 5.9(b). This is the expression of the cdr coding system of a list structure using binary trees. Because we omit one infix functor '|', if the cdr part of that list also has one list structure, we add list tag to this node. This is because we must distinguish [X|Y] from [X,Y]. The double circle in Figure 5.9 (b) is the node to which we add list tag.

(2) Expressions of clauses

One relationship is expressed by one tree. The alternative clause heads are members of one tree, each of them the right-son of another. And each clause body and the clause head are connected to each other. This tree made from all the alternative clauses of one relationship is called a clause tree. For example, there are two relationships 'member' and 'above' shown in Figure 5.10. Their clause trees are shown in Figure 5.9(c).

We show the method of data expressions using DEC-10 style Prolog [Warren 77] in Figure 5.11 to compare the BTM method discussed above with the method of DEC-10 style Prolog, usually the conventional method of data expression. Clearly, in DEC-10 style Prolog, pointers are used to express structured data. But, in the BTM method, we omit all the pointers which point to structured data.

(3) Expressions of environment

For a sequential logic programming system, the environment of execution can be processed by the stack structure efficiently. But for a parallel system, the environment of execution should be structured like a tree. Clearly, if we use BTM method to expressed that tree rather than connecting nodes with pointers, the environment management will be processed more efficiently. The details of this will be discussed in next two chapters.

5.4 Some results of evaluation

BTM method described above has been simulated in a prototype interpreter of P-Prolog. A binary memory is used to keep the source programs in this P-Prolog system. Figure 5.12 shows the instructions of the binary memory manager. As for

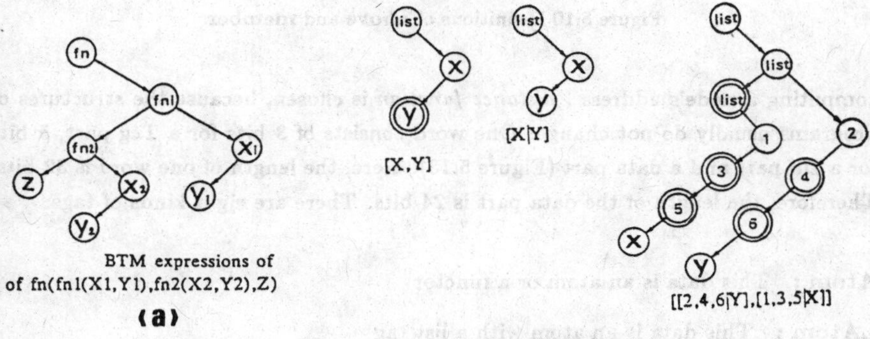

BTM expressions of
of fn(fn1(X1,Y1),fn2(X2,Y2),Z)

(a)

BTM expressions of list

(b)

BTM expressions of clause

(c)

Figure 5.9 BTM Expressions

```
above( X,Y ):- on( X,Y ).
above( X,Z ):- on( X,Y ), above( Y,Z ).

member( X,[X|_] ).
member( X,[_|Y] ):- member( X,Y ).
```

Figure 5.10 Definitions of above and member

computing a node's address , *distance function* is chosen, because the structures of programs usually do not change. One word consists of 3 bits for a Tag part, 5 bits for a Dif part and a data part (Figure 5.13). Here, the length of one word is 32 bits. Therefore, the length of the data part is 24 bits. There are eight kinds of tags:

Atom : This data is an atom or a functor

LAtom : This data is an atom with a list tag

Int : This data is a number

LInt : This data is a number with a list tag

Var : This data is a variable

LVar : This data is a variable with a list tag

Ref : This data is a pointer pointing to a shared structure (This tag is used in the environment stack only)

Point : This data is a pointer except Ref

These tags are used not only for the source program area but also dynamic environments. As shown above, pointers are used here, but they are only used to share variables and structures.

Because Dif has only 5 bits, the limit of the amount of right subtree is 31 nodes. But, we can expand the Dif area as shown in Fig.5.13. If the value of Dif is not equal to zero, we use only two tags : Atom or LAtom. In this case, only 1 bit will be sufficient for tag, and we can expand the Dif area using the left 2 bits in the Tag area. As a result, the limit of the amount of the right subtree becomes 127 nodes. This length of the Dif area is enough to express ordinary Prolog programs.

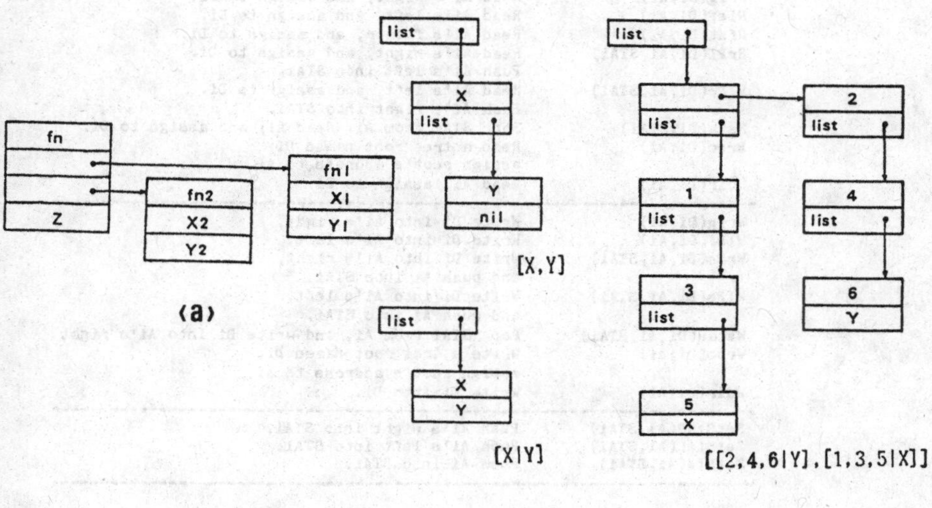

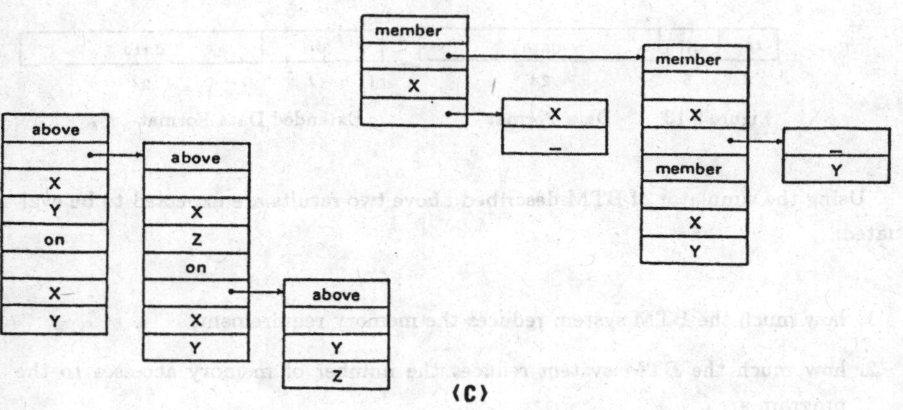

Figure 5.11 DEC-10 Expressions

```
------------------------------------------------------------------------
Rrig(Di,Ai)            Read Ai's right, and assign to Di.
Rlef(Di,Ai)            Read Ai's left, and assign to Di.
Rfat(Di,Ai)            Read Ai's father, and assign to Di.
RrPl(Di,Ai,STAi)       Read Ai's right, and assign to Di.
                       Push Ai's left into STAi.
RlPr(Di,Ai,STAi)       Read Ai's left, and assign to Di.
                       Push Ai's right into STAi.
Rsta(Di,STAi)          Pop  STAi from Ai. Read Ai, and assign to Di.
Rroo(Di,Ai)            Read a tree root named Di,
                       assign root's address to Ai.
Rdir(Di,Ai)            Read Ai, assign to Di.
------------------------------------------------------------------------
Wrig(Di,Ai)            Write Di into Ai's right.
Wlef(Di,Ai)            Write Di into Ai's left.
WrPo(Di,Ai,STAi)       Write Di into Ai's right,
                       and push Ai into STAi.
WlPo(Di,Ai,STAi)       Write Di into Ai's left,
                       and push Ai into STAi.
WstaR(Di,Ai,STAi)      Pop  STAi from Ai, and write Di into Ai's right
Wroo(Di,Ai)            write a tree root named Di,
                       assign root's address to Ai.
Wdir(Di,Ai)            Write Di into Di.
------------------------------------------------------------------------
SetStaR(Ai,STAi)       Push Ai's right into STAi.
SetStaL(Ai,STAi)       Push Ai's left into STAi.
SetSta(Ai,STAi)        Push Ai into STAi.
------------------------------------------------------------------------

          Here, i = 0 or 1.
          Rigister:  D1 and D2  ( for keep data )
          Rigister:  A1 and A2  ( for keep address )
          Stack:     STA1 and STA2
```

Figure 5.12 Instructions of BTM

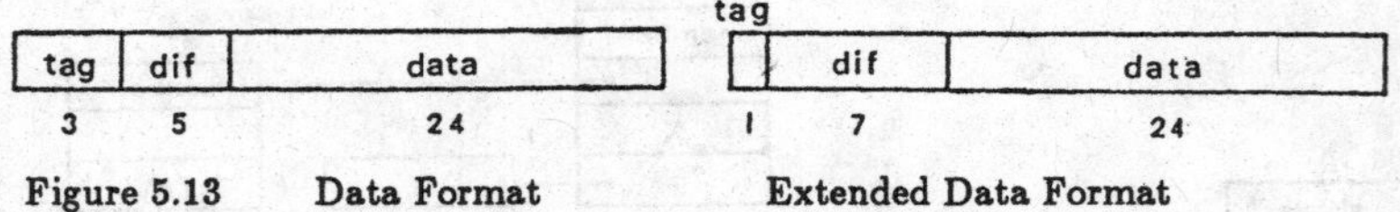

Figure 5.13 Data Format Extended Data Format

Using the simulator of BTM described above two results are expected to be evaluated:

1. how much the BTM system reduces the memory requirement,
2. how much the BTM system reduces the number of memory accesses to the program area.

As described in Section 5.1, the aim of the research about BTM is the efficient processing of tree structured data that is the main object of nonnumeric computation. Considering the example in Figure 5.1 and Figure 5.2 we expect that BTM will reduce the amount of memory access and memory requirement about 40%. But this example includes many nestings of tree structured data. Thus this is a very special case. This evaluation is not valid for many practical programs. Therefore, we have adopted benchmark programs proposed in [Okuno 84] and some practical programs (Table 5.1) as examples for this evaluation.

The results of simulations are given in Table 5.2 and Table 5.3. Table 5.2 is the result of the comparison of the memory requirement. According to this table, we can say that the BTM system can reduce the memory requirement about 20% - 48% compared to DEC-10 style Prolog. Table 5.3 is the comparison of the number of total memory accesses. In this evaluation, we chose structure sharing. According to Table 5.3, we will get results compared with the method of DEC-10 style Prolog with respect to the number of total memory accesses, that is a 17% - 36% reduction.

If we assume that there is hardware that can compute the BTM function rapidly (Figure 5.14 shows an implementation example of BTM), we expect that BTM methods will increase the efficiency of the tree structured data processing which is the basic operation for logic language. It is especially important to reduce the number of memory accesses for the parallel processing model where processors share the program area, because the memory accesses of other processors conflict with each other. And it is very important to reduce the memory requirement for the parallel processing model where processors copy the structured data many times. Those are the advantages to BTM method in terms of developing special architectures. On the other hand, in term of software, it is also an efficient method in respect of environment management, which will be noted in the following chapters.

No.	program name	illustrate
1	Atom-1 Atom-5	Unification of Atom, Arity of one arity of five. For 100 iterations.
	Var-1 Var-5	Unification of variables. Arity of one and arity of five.
	Con-1 Con-5	Unification of constant structure. Arity one and arity five. For 100 iterations.
	Str-1 Str-5	Unification of nonconstant structure. Arity one and arity five. For 100 iterations.
	Str-Var-1 Str-Var-5	Unification of variables with structure. Arity one and arity five. For 100 iterations.
	Var-Str-1 Var-Str-5	Unification of structures with variable. Arity one and arity five. For 100 iterations.
	Det-Call Ndet-Call Shallow-Back Deep-Back	Deterministic simple call Nondeterministic simple call Sallow backtracking Deep backtracking
2	Key-First First Key-Last Last Key-Middle Middle	Database search. Get first clause with primary key, get first clause, get last clause with primary key, get last clause, get middle clause with primary key, and get middle clause. For all of them 100 iterations.
3	Rev-30	List30 naive reverse, for 100 iterations
4	Sort-50	List50 quick sort, for 100 iterations
5	Srev-4 Srev-5	Slow reverse. 4 elements. 5 elements.
6	8-Queen-1 8-Queen-all	Eight queen for one solution. Eight queen for all solution.
7	Deriv	Symbolic differentiation
8	mis	Missionaries and cannibals.
9	parser	A simple parser of English.

Table 5.1 Illustration of Benchmark

No.	spaces in word DEC_10 Prolog (DW)	spaces in word BTM (BW)	ratios (DW-BW)/DW
1	1335	1046	22%
2	1233	984	20%
3	279	159	43%
4	413	216	48%
5	326	233	28%
6	386	308	20%
7	460	355	22%
8	718	555	23%
9	594	453	24%

Table 5.2 Comparison of the Memory Space

No.	program name	DEC-10 Prolog's access times BA	BTM's total access times DA	ratios R = (DA-BA)/DA
1	Atom-1	5928	4720	20%
	Atom-5	6737	5529	18%
	Var-1	5928	4720	20%
	Var-5	6737	5529	18%
	Con-1	6537	5129	22%
	Con-5	9737	7529	23%
	Str-1	6537	5129	22%
	Str-5	9737	7529	23%
	Str-Var-1	6037	4729	22%
	Str-Var-5	8831	7129	19%
	Var-Str-1	6337	5029	21%
	Var-Str-5	8837	7129	19%
	Det-Call	6837	5429	21%
	Ndet-Call	5937	4729	20%
	Shallow-Back	11928	9720	18%
	Deep-Back	25537	21029	18%
2	Key-First	6137	4929	20%
	First	6137	4929	20%
	Key-Last	57429	38721	33%
	Last	111137	92429	17%
	Key-Middle	49337	37329	24%
	Middle	70937	58929	17%
3	Rev-30	10864	8273	24%
4	Sort-50	12303	9350	24%
5	Srev-4	3984	3080	23%
	Srev-5	15679	12165	22%
6	8-Queen-1	127091	102374	19%
	8-Queen-all	2053698	1653499	19%
7	Diff	4665	3086	34%
8	mis	55508	39230	29%
9	parser	543	347	36%

Table 5.3 Comparison of the Access Time

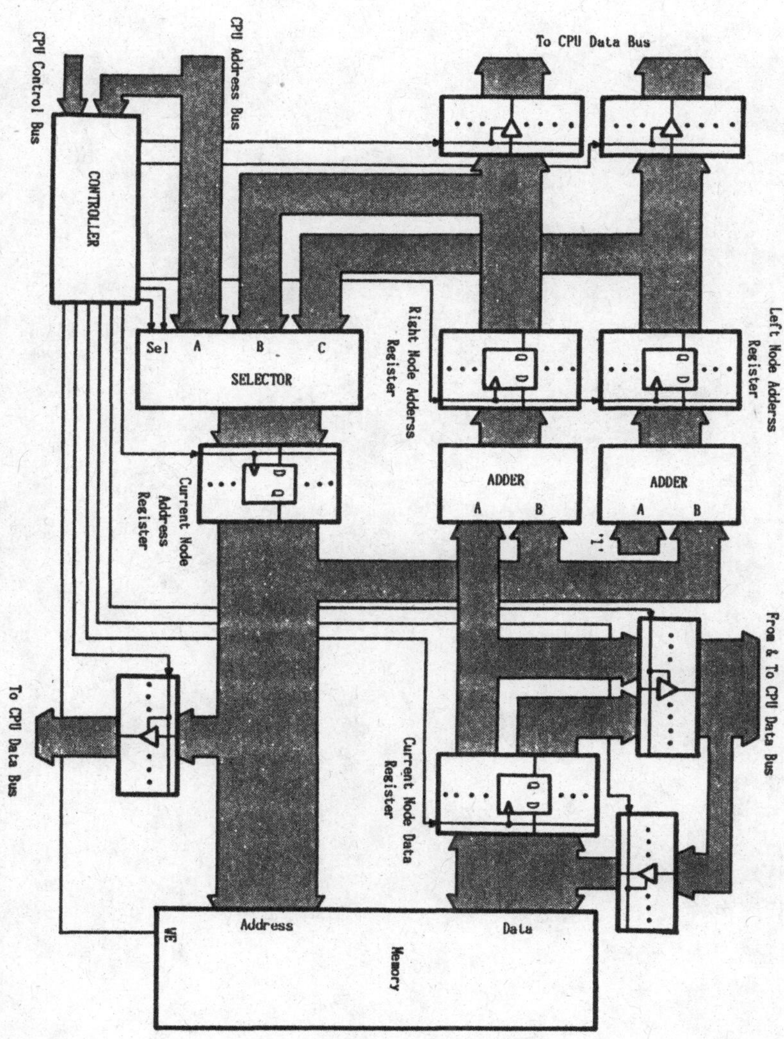

Figure 5.14 An implementation Example of BTM

Chapter 6

Efficient Memory Management for Multiple Environments

As mentioned in Chapter 3, or-parallelism in logic languages means that a goal can be evaluated in parallel when there is more than one alternative clause which can match the goal. As a matter of fact, two kinds of or-parallelism can be classified. In a broad sense, or-parallelism is regarded as a parallel reduction for finding multiple solutions. And in a narrow sense (only for committed choice non-deterministic languages), or-parallelism is regarded as parallelism in which the head unification and a special part of the body named the guard are executed in parallel, but only one clause is selected for reduction. Because the latter cannot find multiple solutions, we call the former "strong" or-parallelism and the latter "weak" or-parallelism. From an implementation viewpoint, the difference between these two kinds of or-parallelism is that the multiple environments must be permanently constructed in strong or-parallelism, whereas they are just temporarily used for reducing one clause in weak or-parallelism.

Weak or-parallelism can be implemented very simply provided that the language is safe or is flat. A safe committed choice non-deterministic language is defined as such a language which can guarantee that the binding of a variable of the goal never occurs before commitment. And a flat one refers to a language of guarded Horn clauses whose guards contain only built-in predicates. The efforts to develop flat or safe language can avoid multiple environments processing so that we can obtain good results with regard to efficiency.

For strong or-parallelism, multiple environments processing can not be avoided. How to manage multiple environments efficiently is an important problem. This chapter presents two efficient memory management methods for multiple environment processing. A scheme named *index binding* is described and compared to existing schemes in Section 6.2. Another scheme named *concentrative binding*, a refinement of *index binding*, is described in Section 6.3. The *concentrative binding* scheme is used in P-Prolog's implementation.

6.1 Related Work

Multiple environments processing is necessary if a variable of the goal may be separately bound to different terms when a goal is unified with more than one alternative clause in parallel. The simplest scheme to solve this problem is to make separate copies of the goal's arguments for each alternative clause, but this is very inefficient. To reduce the copying overhead, variant schemes based on the idea of shared environments have been proposed.

(1) Demand Driven Copying:

In this scheme, an argument is copied only when an attempt is made to instantiate it, so that only necessary information is copied [Levy 84]. Though this scheme minimizes copying, its mechanism is rather complicated, so it is the slowest one compared with the other schemes.

(2) Deep Binding:

In contrast to the idea of copying, binding a variable to several local environments has been considered. A primitive binding scheme named deep binding is described in [Satou *et al.* 84]. The basic idea is based on making a special area (called an association list or a hash window) for each independent environment to store the local values of variables. If or-parallel execution attempts to bind a variable to more than one term, then the address of the variable and its binding will be kept in the local association list separately. The problem with this scheme is that to access a local binding a linear search from the current association list towards ancestor association lists is necessary.

(3) Shallow Binding:

Instead of deep binding, a more efficient scheme is proposed in [Miyazaki *et al.* 85]. This scheme uses the "trail cell" to record information for a variable which needs a local binding. Such information includes the current value of the variable and the old value of the variable. By searching the trail cells, accessing a local binding is much faster than the deep binding scheme because a linear search is not necessary.

(4) Binding Array:

Another binding scheme which is similar to the deep binding scheme was simultaneously proposed in [Warren 84]. To overcome the cost of linear searching, a binding array (called BA) is introduced. In theory, for each environment there is a BA which records all local bindings of all ancestor environments so that local bindings can be accessed immediately. If a BA is actually constructed for every new environment, it is very inefficient. For this reason, Warren presents an optimization in which a BA is dynamically constructed. According to a rough estimate, to access a local binding, the overhead of dynamically constructing a BA is rather more expensive than searching the trail cells [Miyazaki *et al.* 85].

(5) Variable Importation:

In this scheme, all unbound variables in the parent environment are imported into the child environment [Lindstrom 84]. The advantage of this scheme is the locality of reference, but its processing speed is slower [Crammond 85].

6.2 An Index Binding scheme

We first present a scheme that can process multiple environments more efficiently than the other schemes described in Section 6.1. It is based on a binding-like scheme. Like [Satou *et al.* 84] and [Warren 84], in this scheme every environment has a hash table (it is called "forward list" in [Warren 84], and "association list" in [Satou *et al.* 84]) for storing the local bindings of variables. But it differs in the methods for managing a local binding (Figure 6.1). To clarify this discussion, we will introduce the following definition:

Definition 6.1: For a variable X which is shared by multiple environments, its original value cell is called X's *global cell*, and its local binding cell in the hash table is called X's *local cell.*

In [Satou *et al.* 84] and [Warren 84], if a variable X in an ancestor environment becomes bound, X's global cell in the ancestor environment is not changed; instead, the pair consisting the X and its local value is added to a hash table of the current environment. For example, considering X and Y to be unified, X is "undef" and Y has bound to a atom keio (Figure 6.1 (a)). In conventional binding schemes, after X unified with Y, X's global cell is still "undef", X's local value "atom:keio" is recorded in a hash table (Figure 6.1 (b)). In our index binding scheme, we do the same work of recording the local binding in a hash table, but we change the global cell of X as shown in Figure 6.1 (c). An extra tag called "shared" is introduced to indicate a variable which has at least local instance binding. An integer which represents the current *generation order number* (defined below) is recorded with the "shared" tag. This integer plays an important role in accessing a local binding quickly.

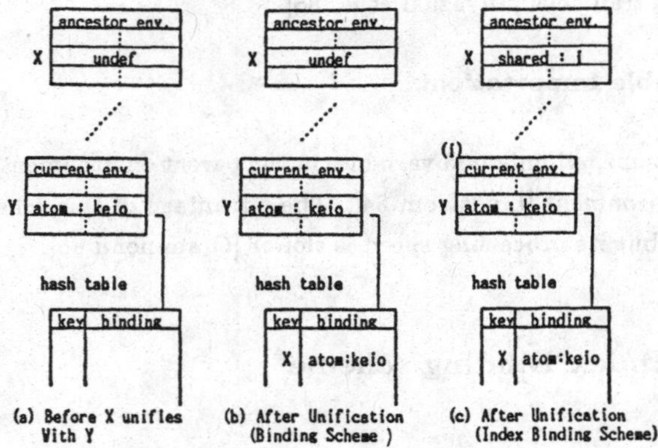

Figure 6.1 Difference Between the Binding Scheme and the Index Binding Scheme

6.2.1 Data Structure and Data Format

The system is constructed by an or-tree in this scheme. Every node in an or-tree has a *generation order number* defined as follows:

Definition 6.2: For a tree **T**,

1. the root's *generation order number* is 0, and
2. if a node's *generation order number* is *d*, then all of its children nodes' *generation order number* is *d+1*.

We will call a *generation order number* a *depth* for short. If a node's *generation order number* is *d*, we call it a *d*-generation node.

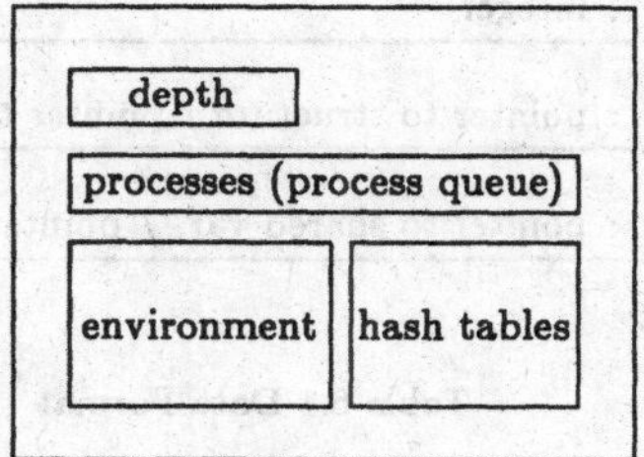

Figure 6.2 A Node in An Or-tree

Every node is made up of four elements, namely, a process, an environment of the process, a hash table, and the depth of this node (Figure 6.2). The environment keeps the value of variables of this process, and the hash table keeps the local value of the variables of the ancestor processes. An item in the hash table is composed of the variable's name, which is the key, and the variable's local value. The following are the different kinds of variable values:

undef: unbound

shared: shared by multiple local environments

atom: bound to an atom

int: bound to an integer

struc: bound to a structure

ref: bound to a variable

Their data format is shown in Table 6.1.

undef	: depth
shared	: depth
atom	: pointer to atom's string
int	: integer
struc	: pointer to structure / pointer to structure's frame
ref	: pointer to shared var. / pointer to hash table (if it exists)

Table 6.1 Data Format

Besides introducing a new kind of data type, "shared", as mentioned above, we also introduce a concept of *reference cell* which is defined as follows.

Definition 6.3: While fetching a variable X's value, if X's value is "ref:p", we should follow pointer to dereference **p** until a term (i.e. "atom", "int", "undef" or "struc") is found. In this case, the first cell of "ref:p" is called the *reference cell* of X's value. Otherwise, if X's value is not "ref:p", we say X has no reference cell.

6.2.2 Algorithm

Binding Algorithm

During unification, our binding algorithm works as follows (Figure 6.3). In case 1 shown in Figure 6.3 (a), because X is not a variable in the ancestor node, local binding is not necessary. If X is not unified with an instance (case 3 and case 4), conventional binding of variables occurs. If X is not in the current environment, a local binding will be made (case 2). The local binding algorithm is shown in Figure 6.3(b). The main work is to write X's local binding into the current hash table. When X has a reference cell (see Definition 6.3), we should save the current hash table's pointer in this cell. After the local binding, X's global cell will change from "undef" to "shared:i", or from "shared:j" to "shared:k" (here $k = \min(i,j)$). "shared:i" indicates that X is now shared by successor nodes, and for all the nodes whose hash table keeps X's local value, whose depths are greater than or equal to i.

Dereferencing Algorithm

Dereferencing occurs when a variable's value cell is "ref : p". In Prolog systems, the dereferencing algorithm is very simple. To access the value of a variable, it repeatedly follows the pointers **p** until a non-ref value is reached. Because a binding between two "undef" obeys a rule described in Figure 6.3 (case 3 and case 4), only one step is in fact necessary. For an or-parallel Prolog system, the dereferencing algorithm becomes complex because of processing local bindings. Our dereferencing algorithm is described as below (Figure 6.4).

When a variable X is indicated by "shared : j", a special dereferencing for a local value starts. First we check the depth of the current node. When it is j, we can immediately find out X's value according to the current hash table. In this case, if there is no local binding in the current hash table, X is unbound. This is because "shared : j" implies that X's value can not possibly be stored in other nodes' hash tables whose depth is greater than j. If the current depth is less than j, we can judge that X is unbound for the same reason as above. If the current depth is greater than j, we will check whether or not X has a reference cell in which a pointer of the hash

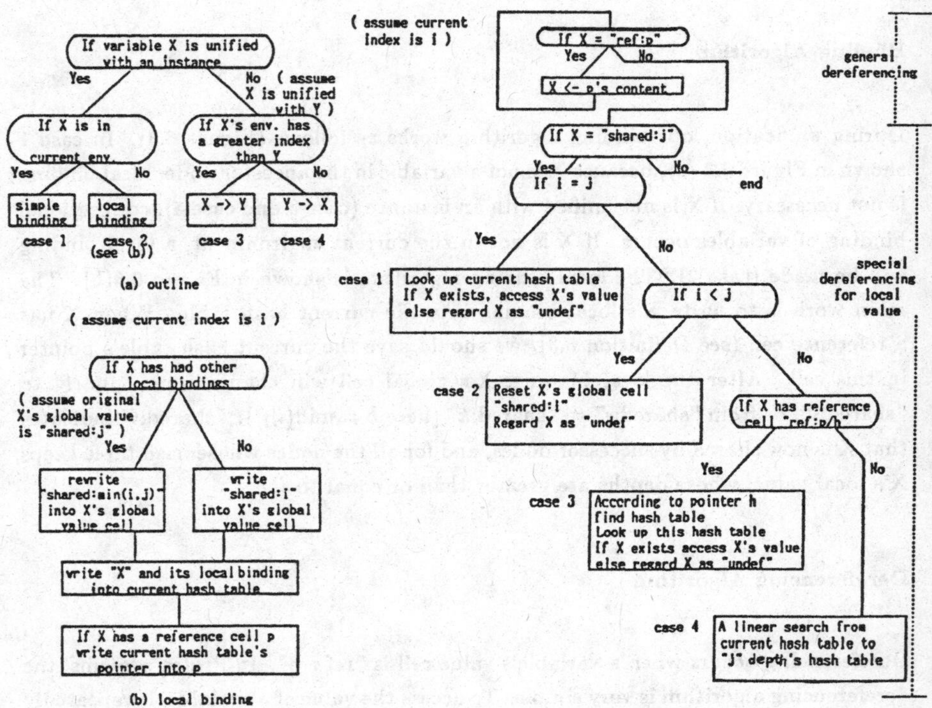

Figure 6.3 Binding Algorithm

Figure 6.4 Dereferencing Algorithm

table is kept. If the answer is yes, we can directly check the hash table pointed to. Otherwise it is necessary to look up the hash tables between the current node and the *j*-generation node (an ancestor).

6.2.3 Comparison

The index binding scheme is here compared with the binding array scheme [Warren 84] and the shallow binding scheme [Miyazaki *et al.* 85], which are considered to be rather efficient schemes. First, the cost of binding is discussed. Then we will mainly compare the dereferencing algorithm.

For the binding algorithm, the differences between the index binding scheme, the shallow binding scheme and the binding array scheme are few. When local binding occurs, each of the three schemes does the following things:

index binding: Write the local binding into the current hash table, write the value (shared : depth) into the variable's value cell, and if X has a reference cell write a pointer to the current hash table in it.

binding array: Write the local binding into the current hash table.

shallow binding: Write the local binding into the right hand of the trail cell, and save the original binding in the left hand of the trail cell.

The binding array scheme is fastest, while our scheme is the most complex. But this difference can be ignored when we evaluate the total cost of binding and dereferencing, since the most difficult problem is how to dereference a local binding quickly.

To compare the three dereferencing algorithms, we first give some abstract execution examples to explain the differences between the schemes. A program is given in Figure 6.5. Four different cases in the execution of goal ?- g(...,X...) are shown from Figure 6.6 to Figure 6.9.

(a) case 1

First assume a process is working in node **n10**, and X has had a local binding in the node **n11** (Figure 6.6). At this time, the three schemes access the X's local value in node **n10** separately in the following ways:

index binding: As shown in Figure 6.4 (case 1), we just check whether X is in the current hash table or not.

binding Array: In this scheme, we check the hash tables from **n10** to root **n1** (namely **n10**, **n4**, **n2** and **n1**). When all of the nodes listed above contain no binding, we are confident that X is "undef" here.

```
g(...,X,...):- s1(...,X,...),... .
g(...,X,...):- s2(...,X,...),... .

s1(...,X,...):- s11(...,X,...),... .
s1(...,X,...):- s12(...,X,...),... .
s1(...,X,...):- s13(...,X,...),... .

s2(...,X,...):- s21(...,X,...),... .
s2(...,X,...):- ...,X = g,... .

s11(...,X,...):- ...,X = a,... .
s11(...,X,...):- ...,X = b,... .

s12(...,X,...):- ...,X = c,... .
s12(...,X,...):- ...,X = d,... .

s13(...,X,...):- ...,X = e,... .
s13(...,X,...):- ...,X = f,... .

s21(...,X,...):- ...,X = h, s211(...,X,...),... .
s21(...,X,...):- ...,X = i,... .

s211(...,X,...):- s2111(...,X,...),... .
s211(...,X,...):- s2112(...,X,...),... .

s2111(...,X,...):- s21111(...,X,...),... .
s2111(...,X,...):- s21112(...,X,...),... .
```

Figure 6.5 An Abstract Example

<u>**shallow binding:**</u> In this scheme, dereferencing does not occur during unification, but during the environment switch. The overhead of dereferencing depends on the distance between the currently active process and the process which should be scheduled next. If we assume that before node **n10**'s process starts, node **n11** was active, then environment switching is executed in the following way. Along with the path from **n11** to **n10** (except **n2**), we check whether or not there are some trail cells. Any pair of trail cells found during this check will be exchanged.

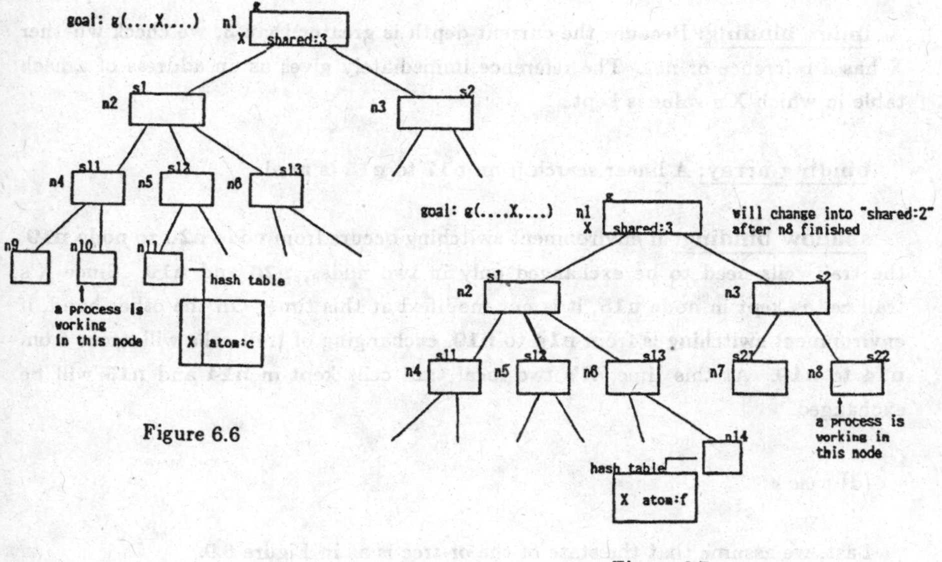

Figure 6.6

Figure 6.7

(b) case 2:

Next, we assume that a process is working in node **n8**. The state of the or-tree is like Figure 6.7.

<u>**index binding:**</u> Because the current depth is less than 3, X's local value is regarded as "undef" without any searching. X's global cell in node **n1** will be modified to "shared:3".

<u>**binding array:**</u> As in case 1, a linear search from the current node to the root is needed.

shallow binding: Environment switching is needed.

(c) case 3:

Now, we assume that a process is working in node **n19**. The state of the or-tree is shown in Figure 6.8. In this case, X's local value for **n19** is kept in node **n15**. To dereference X, the three schemes proceed as follows.

index binding: Because the current depth is greater than 3, we check whether X has a reference or not. The reference immediately gives us an address of a hash table in which X's value is kept.

binding array: A linear search from **n17** to **n15** is need.

shallow binding: If environment switching occurs from node **n20** to node **n19**, the trail cells need to be exchanged only in two nodes, **n20** and **n19**. Since X's trail cell is kept in node **n15**, it is not modified at this time. On the other hand, if environment switching is from **n14** to **n19**, exchanging of trail cells will occur from **n14** to **n19**. At this time, X's two local trail cells kept in **n14** and **n15** will be exchanged.

(d) case 4:

Last, we assume that the state of the or-tree is as in Figure 6.9.

index binding: Since the current depth is greater than 2 and there is no hash table pointer kept in X's reference cell, we must look up the hash table from **n9** to **n4** (namely **n9** and **n4**). Linear searching is needed in our scheme only in a case like this one.

binding array: This scheme needs to look up the hash tables, but it must search all hash table from the current node to the root.

shallow binding: Environment switching is needed.

A comparison result is summaried in Figure 6.10, in which we regard the cost

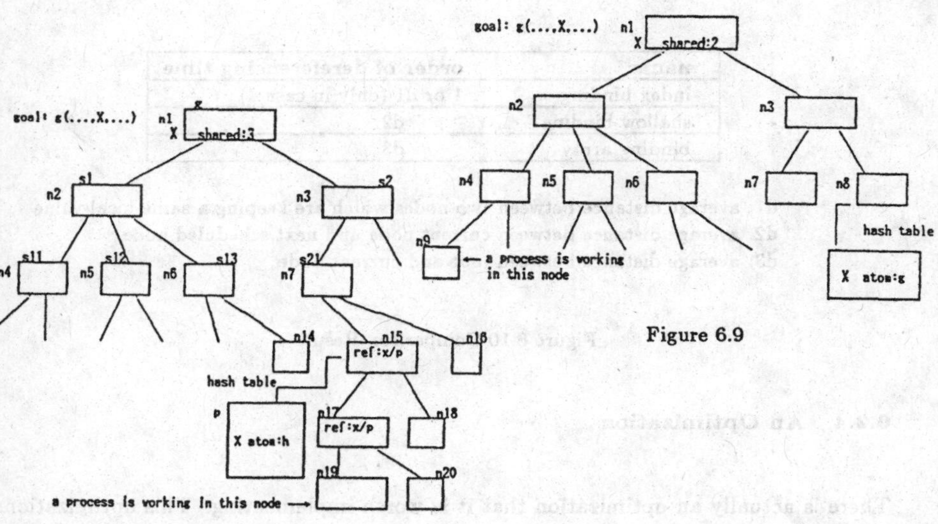

Figure 6.8

Figure 6.9

of one step of searching as 1. According to the index binding's algorithm (Figure 6.4) and the comparison discussed above, it is clearly that the cost for dereferencing a local value of variable X is only 1 except for case 4. But, the costs of others schemes are d2 (average distance between current node to next scheduled node) and d3 (average distance between root to current node). As for case 4 in Figure 6.4, the index binding scheme costs d1 (average distance between two nodes which are keeping same variable's local values). It is commonly the case that

$$d1 \leq d2 \leq d3.$$

Therefore the index scheme is the most efficient one compared with the others. This is because the special tag "shared" and reference cell are introduced.

name	order of dereferencing time
index binding	1 or d1 (only in case 4)
shallow binding	d2
binding array	d3

d1: average distance between two nodes which are keeping a same local value
d2: average distance between current node and next scheduled node
d3: average distance between root and current node

Figure 6.10 Comparison Result

6.2.4 An Optimization

There is actually an optimization that it is worth implementing. This optimization processes reference cells in a different way. During a local binding (Figure 6.3 (b)), if the variable X has a reference cell **p**, we can write X's local binding into cell **p**, instead of writing a hash table's pointer. As a result, the case 3 in dereference algorithm (Figure 6.4) will not occur. The advantages of this optimization are not only to speed up the dereferencing, but also to decrease the access frequency of the hash tables. The latter is very important when we consider using a shared memory to keep the hash tables.

6.3 Concentrative Binding Scheme

In this section, another memory management method is presented. It is based on the index binding scheme described above, but it uses a different method for managing the local bindings of variables. The index binding scheme and the other schemes such as [Miyazaki *et al.* 85] and [Warren 84] have something in common: that they distribute local bindings to every local environment. The advantage of the distributing policy is that every local value of a variable can be accessed in parallel when the system is built on a multi-processor machine. In this kind of scheme, the accessing method is supported in the order bottom up. This means that a local value of a variable X can be obtained only when a process in this local environment wants to dereference X.

If a process in an ancestor node needs to collect all the local bindings of X, either the cost will be very expensive or the collection is almost impossible. This is because there is no top down accessing method supported in those schemes. A top down accessing is considered necessary if the system is expected to execute predicates such as **setof** and **bagof** fast or to combine and-parallelism and or-parallelism efficiently. For this reason, we propose a concentrative binding scheme in which local bindings of variables are not distributed but collected together.

6.3.1 Main Differences Between Concentrative and Index Binding Schemes

Instead of making a hash table for every local environment, we make a hash table for every variable which is shared by multiple local environments. In this scheme, the structure of the or-tree is the same as that in index binding except for the hash table. The data format is also similar to the index binding scheme. During a local binding for variable X, we will write the name of the current node (defined in the next section) and X's local binding into X's hash table (Figure 6.11). The name of a node is used as a key of the node's local value of X. To dereference X, we use the same policy as depth checking. The only thing that must be modified in the dereferencing is the method of looking for the hash table, because it is constructed in a different way.

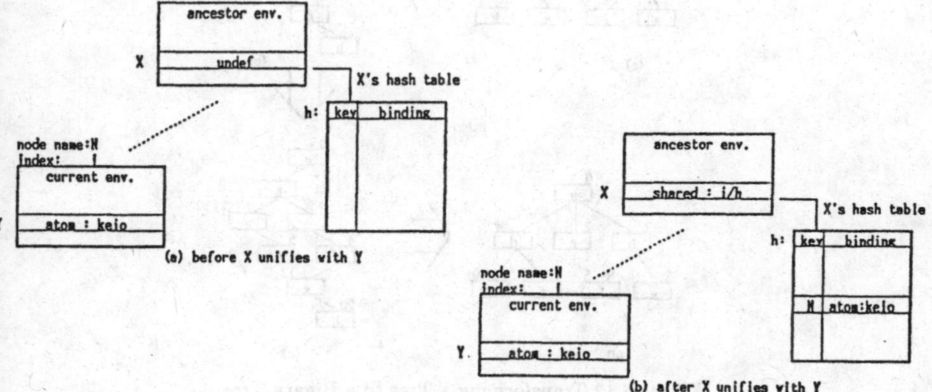

Figure 6.11 The Concentrative Binding Scheme

6.3.2 Coding the Nodes

The most important problem is how to name a node, since the name of a node is a key to a local value in a variable's hash table. The node's name should indicate its position in an or-tree and its relation with other nodes clearly. Here, we discuss a naming method which is based on a suggestion from binary tree memory described in Chapter 5.

First, the or-tree is transformed into a binary tree in the following way (also see Figure 5.3):

Definition 6.4: For any arbitrary tree **T**, its transformed binary tree **Tb** is a binary tree such that

1. **Tb**'s root is **T**'s root;
2. for a node in **Tb**, its right son, the right son's left son, the right son's left son's left son, ... and so on, are children of the corresponding node in **T**.

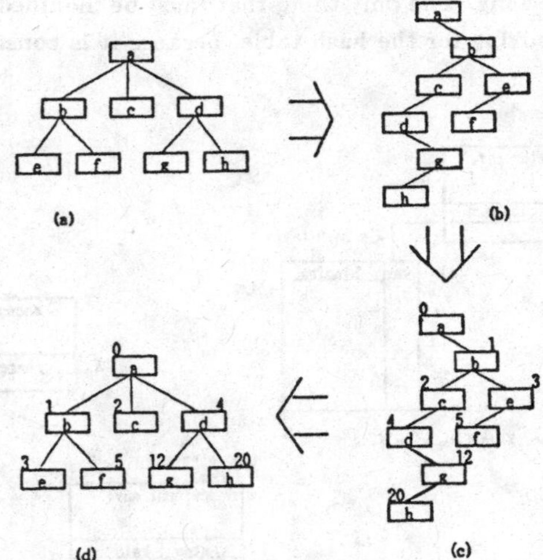

Figure 6.12 Transforming a Tree to a Binary Tree

We can simply say that a right-son in **Tb** represents a parent-child relation of **T**, and a left-son in **Tb** represents a brother relation of **T**. The tree shown in Figure 6.12 (a) will be transformed into a binary tree shown in Figure 6.12 (b) by using Definition 6.4.

After transforming **T** into **Tb**, we give every node of **Tb** a number as its code according to the breakdown function described in Section 5.2. Using this function (Formula 5.2), the binary tree shown in Figure 6.12 (b) is coded like Figure 6.12 (c). As a result, the original or-tree will be coded like Figure 6.12 (d).

The breakdown function gives the parent-child relation in a binary tree, but it does not directly express the parent-child relation in the original arbitrary tree. Therefore another formula derived from the breakdown function is given below.

For any arbitrary tree **T**, if its transformed binary tree **Tb** is coded by using the breakdown function, then for any node n in **T**, its parent-child relation can be expressed by using the following formula:

$$child(n, depth) = \begin{cases} n + 2^{depth+1} \\ n + 2^{depth+2} \\ n + 2^{depth+3} \\ \vdots \\ \vdots \end{cases} \quad (6.1.a)$$

$$parent(n, depth) = n - 2^{depth} \qquad (6.1.b)$$

Node that the depth used here is **Tb**'s depth, not **T**'s depth.

Formula 6.1 can be simply proven as follows.

proof:

(a) According to Definition 6.4 (definition of the transformed binary tree) for any node n of tree **T**, its children are those nodes which are n's right-son, n's right-son's left-son, ... and so on in **Tb**. Applying the breakdown function to the above statement, we obtain

$$child(n, depth) \in \{n + 2^{depth+1},\ n + 2^{depth+2}, ...\}$$

(here, *depth* is *n*'s depth in **Tb**)

(b) According to Definition 6.4 and the breakdown function, node *n*'s parent can be obtained by calculating *n*'s parent in **Tb** until the first right node in **Tb** is found. If *n* is a right node in **Tb** and its depth in **Tb** is *depth*, then we have

$$parent(n, depth) = father(n, depth) = n - 2^{depth}$$

so Formula 6.1.*b* holds for *n* in this case.

Assuming Formula 6.1.*b* holds for *n*, which is a right node in **Tb**, and its index in **Tb** is *depth*, we prove that Formula 6.1.*b* also holds for *m* which is the left-son of *n* in **Tb** as follows.

$$\begin{array}{lll}
\because & (1)\ parent(n, depth) = n - 2^{depth} & (assumed\ above) \\
\because & (2)\ father(m, depth + 1) = m - 2^{depth} = n & (according\ to\ Formula\ 5.2) \\
\because & (3)\ m\ and\ n\ are\ brothers\ in\ \mathbf{T} & \\
\therefore & parent(m, depth + 1) & \\
= & parent(n, depth) & \\
= & n - 2^{depth} & (applying(1)) \\
= & m - 2^{depth} - 2^{depth} & (applying(2)) \\
= & m - 2^{depth+1} &
\end{array}$$

□

6.3.3 Implementation of Concentrative Binding Scheme

We use the coding method described above to code an or-tree. Every node retains its code and two depths (the original tree's depth and transformed tree's depth). We call the original tree's depth *depth*, and the transformed binary tree's depth *module* for distinction. A node's name is composed of its *code* and its *module*, namely (*code,module*). As mentioned in Section 6.3.1, when a variable X in an ancestor node becomes bound, X's local binding is written in X's hash table with a key (*code,module*) which is the current node's name. This not only means that X is bound in this node, but also indicates that this local binding is valid for all the nodes whose name (*c,m*) satisfies

$$c \bmod 2^{module} = code \qquad (6.2).$$

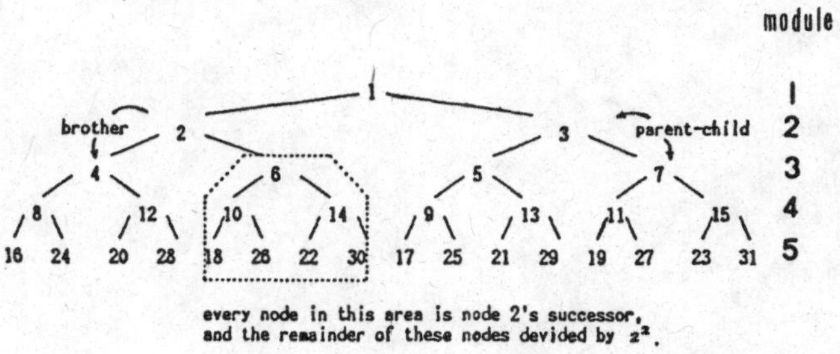

Figure 6.13 Relation Between nodes

Formula 6.2 is very useful when we want to check whether two nodes are in the ancestor-successor relation (Figure 6.13).

While dereferencing variable X, we use the node's name to look for X's hash table. If a linear search is necessary (case 4 described in Figure 6.4), we use Formula 6.1 to calculate the parent node's name. The cost of this scheme is of the same order as the index scheme, since the two schemes are based on the same depth checking method.

There is another problem which should be mentioned here. According to the coding method described in Section 6.3.2, it is clear that a node's code will grow along with the expansion of the or-tree's size. For this reason, a node's name is a variable-length word. In the hash table, a node's name is used as a key, so we hope it is a fixed-length word for the sake of efficiency. To solve this problem, we do not write the real code of a node into a hash table in our implementation. Instead, we just write a difference which is obtained by subtracting the current node's code from the ancestor's code. In this way, a fixed-length word is enough to represent a key, because the distance between a variable and its local binding is not very far.

The concentrative binding scheme looks rather complicated, but it has the important advantage of collecting a variable's local bindings efficiently. It is very effective for combining and-parallelism and or-parallelism, because the sending of all the local bindings to another process is often required in such a computational model.

We are now using the concentrative binding scheme to implement P-Prolog.

Chapter 7

Combining And-parallelism and Or-parallelism

This chapter presents a scheme of combining *and*- and *or*- parallelism, which is being practically implemented for P-Prolog.

7.1 Difficulty in Combining *and*- and *or*- Parallelism

Here, we give an example to explain the problems that occur in the implementation of both kinds of parallelism.

```
program intersect

(1) intersect( X,L1,L2,L3 ): -
        member( X,L1 ), member( X,L2 ), member( X,L3 ).

(2) member( X,[X|_] ): - true.
(3) member( X,[_|Y] ): - member( X,Y ).
```

First, suppose that the goal statement is ?- intersect(A,[1,2,3],[3,4,5],[9,6,3]).

An and-or parallel execution procedure of an intersect program listed below is

shown in Figure 7.1.

As shown in Figure 7.1, after **intersect(A,[1,2,3],[3,4,5],[9,6,3])** is reduced to **member(A,[1,2,3])**, **member(A,[3,4,5])** and **member(A,[9,6,3])**, the variable A becomes shared by the three goals. Since the three goals are executed in parallel, we usually consider every goal has its own local A temporarily, and find a set of compatible solutions after all of A's local values are obtained. Figure 7.2 shows the bindings obtained from a consistency check between {1,2,3}, {3,4,5} and {9,6,3}. This kind of execution procedure is based on pure Horn clauses and is used to combine *full-and-* parallelism and *or* parallelism. From this simple example, we can see that the execution of this kind of parallelism is very inefficient, because of the following two principal weaknesses:

1. First, the cost of the consistency check will take $o(N_1 \times ... \times N_m)$, where m is the number of or-branches, and N_i is the number of solutions obtained from one or-branch.

2. Since inconsistency can not be determined until all the solutions return back from the or-branches, many redundant searches will occur, and that will cause a danger of explosion of the search space. For example, suppose the goal statement is

   '... **intersect(A,[1,2,3],[3,4,5],[9,6,3])**,..., **A = 1** '. Even though **A = 1** can make a binding of A quickly, the consistency check can not occur until another local value of A is bound by the goal of **intersect**.

Therefore, to combine *full-and-* and *or-* parallelism, we must solve the above problems.

There have been several efforts to try this combination. Pollard proposed a scheme for and-or proof procedure in his dissertation [Pollard 81]. In this scheme, every set of solutions from an or-branch will pass through a **filter** which plays the role of consistency check. The above problems were not solved by Pollard's scheme. According to [Syre and Westphal 85], Kasif and Minker, Spacek and Petros also proposed schemes for combining both *and-* and *or-* parallelism separately. In Kasif and Minker's proposal, two operators **UNIF** (for consistency check) and **MERGE** (for collecting multiple solutions) are introduced into and-nodes and or-nodes respectively. A merit

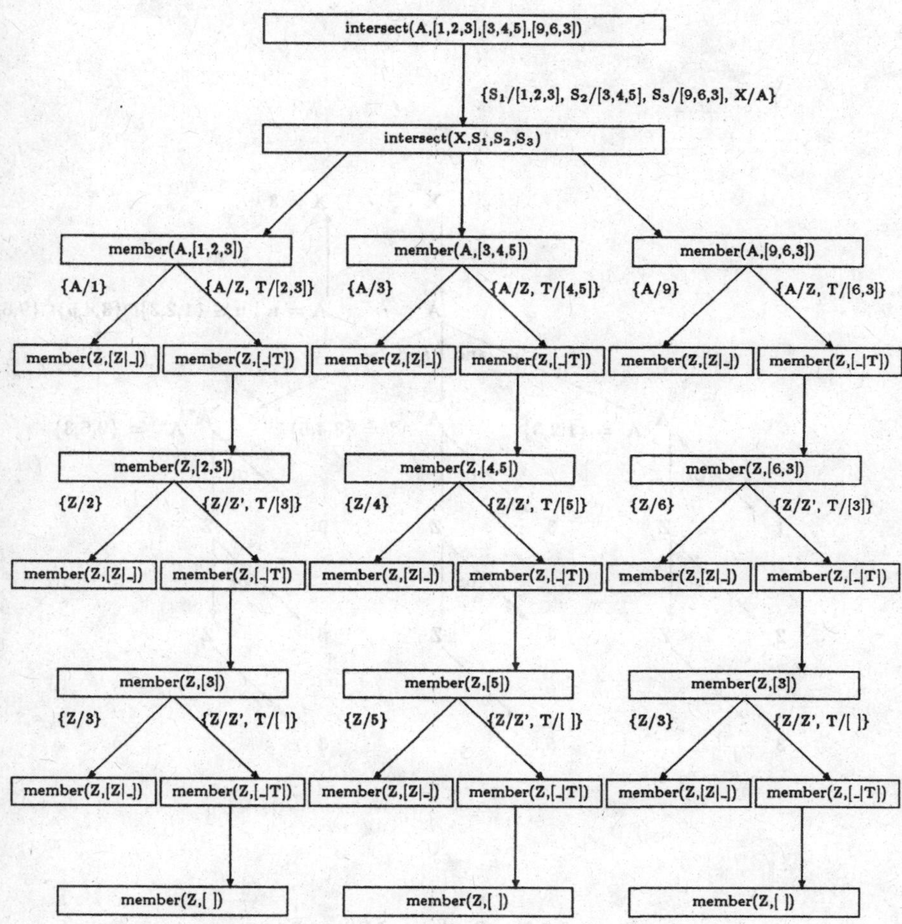

Figure 7.1 An And-or Parallel Execution Procedure of Intersect Program

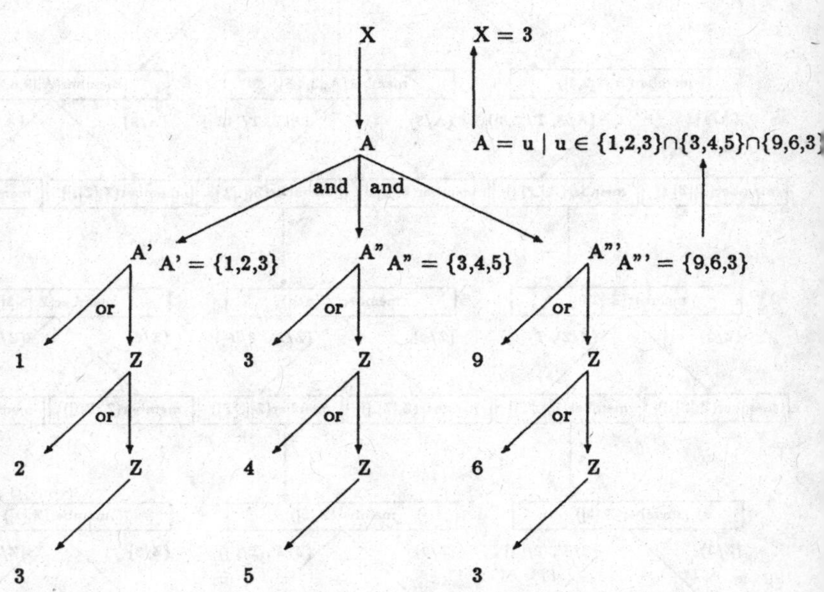

Figure 7.2 The Bindings of Figure 7.1

of their scheme is that the system will detect related and-nodes immediately when an or-node obtains an empty list from MERGE operator so that the explosion of the search space can be reduced somewhat. As for Spacek and Petros's proposal, it also has the advantage of reducing the search space, and it has another improvement about consistency check: the check is executed only between two *and* goals which have at least one variable shared by them. Anyway, all of the proposals above still share the basic idea of consistency check. Therefore, there may also be a problem in respect of efficiency.

There is another approach which combines not *full-and-* parallelism, but *and-* parallelism (that means *stream-and-* and *restricted and-* parallelism) with *or*-parallelism The problem for this combination is how to efficiently process the incremental communication between a goal which produces multiple solutions and another goal which accepts those solutions. To our knowledge there has been no scheme for this kind of combination published yet.

7.2 An Outline of the Implementation of P-Prolog

Facing the difficulty described above, we present a scheme to combine *and-* parallelism and *or-* parallelism.

In this scheme:

1. the consistency check method is avoided,
2. the communication problem can be solved in a reasonably efficient manner.

The scheme is used to implement not pure Horn clauses but the extended guarded Horn clauses, namely, *classified Horn clauses.* This is the reason why we can avoid a consistency check. Since the scheme is restricted to only combine *and-* parallelism and *or-* parallelism, we can say that for every variable shared between goals there exists only one goal (called the producer) which has the right to bind this variable. The other goals sharing this variable (called consumers) just receive the results of the binding from that goal.

To solve the communication problem, two novel types of variable, *or-shared* and *communicator*, are introduced.

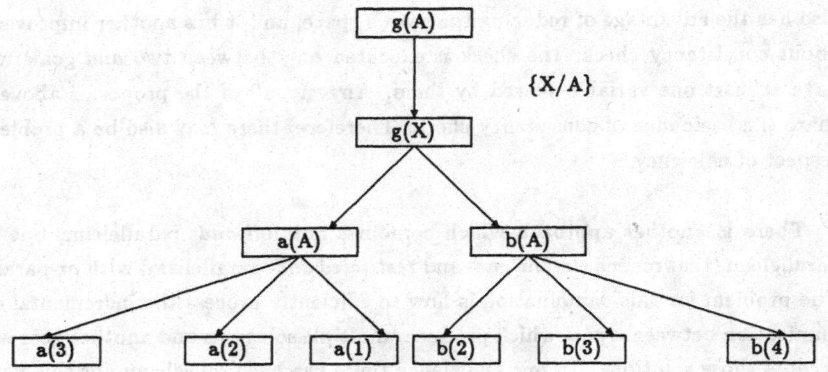

Figure 7.3 An Execution Model in *Full-and/or* Parallelism

An introductory example is described and compared with the conventional scheme here in order to give an outline of our scheme. The following is a simple problem written in both Prolog (Horn clauses) and P-Prolog (classified Horn clauses):

program (in Prolog)

```
(1)     g( X ):- a( X ), b( X ).

(2)     a( 3 ).
(3)     a( 2 ).
(4)     a( 1 ).

(5)     b( 2 ).
(6)     b( 3 ).
(7)     b( 4 ).
```

program (in P-Prolog)

```
(1)   g( X ): - a( X ), b( X ).

(2)   a( 3 ): -- true.
(3)   a( 2 ): -- true.
(4)   a( 1 ): -- true.

(5)   b( 2 ).
(6)   b( 3 ).
(7)   b( 4 ).
```

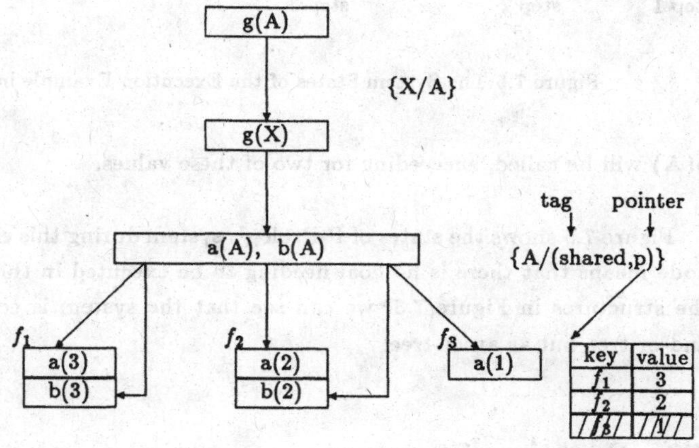

Figure 7.4 The Execution Model in P-Prolog

Suppose we have a goal **?- g(A)**. Its execution procedure by a *full-and-/or* parallelism scheme is shown in Figure 7.3. Figure 7.4 shows its execution procedure by P-Prolog's implementation. Comparing Figure 7.3 with Figure 7.4, we can see that they work in different ways. P-Prolog does not execute **a(A)** and **b(A)** in *full-and-*parallel. Since all of the alternative clauses defined for **b** are single neck clauses, **b(A)** can not be reduced until **A** becomes bound. Therefore, **a(A)** is reduced first. According to P-Prolog's implementation scheme, because **a(A)** is reduced by *double clauses*, it returns a 'value' (**shared:** *p*) etc. for variable **A**. As noted in Section 6.2.3, **shared** is a tag to indicate **A** is an *or-shared* variable, and *p* is a pointer to **A**'s hash table. At the next step, for each local value of **A** placed in table *p* by **a(A)**,

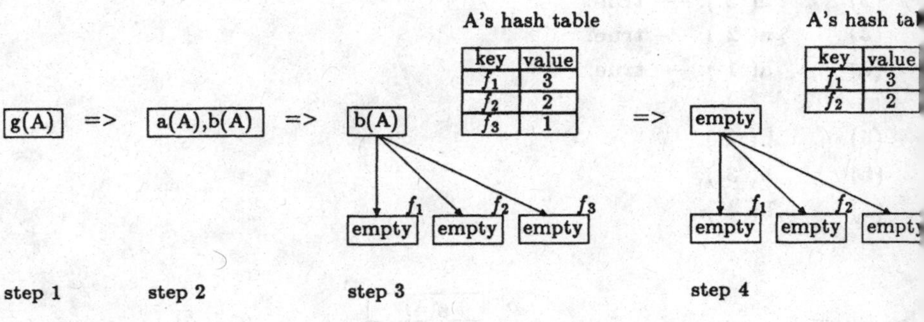

Figure 7.5 The System States of the Execution Example in Figure 7.4

b(A) will be called, succeeding for two of these values.

Figure 7.5 shows the states of P-Prolog's system during this execution. The *empty* node means that there is no goal needing to be executed in this node. Referring to the structures in Figure 7.5, we can see that the system is constructed not as an and-or tree but as an or-tree.

7.3 Run-time Structure

This section explains the run-time structure of P-Prolog in a top-down way. Even though some contents have been described in Chapter 6 briefly, we will review them in detail here.

The system is made up of three kinds of components:

- a source program area
- an or-tree
- a set of hash tables

7.3.1 Source Program Area

The source program area is used to keep source programs. In this area, P-Prolog's programs are stored as binary tree expressions, as described in Chapter 5.

7.3.2 Or-tree

The or-tree is used to record the dynamic state of the execution. Every node in the or-tree is composed of:

1. an *and* queue,
2. an environment (one or more frames),
3. a trail list, and
4. node's information.

The composition of a node is summarized in Figure 7.6.

The *and* queue contains all of the goals which have not executed yet. The structure of an *and* queue is shown in Figure 7.6 (a). Each element of the queue is just a pair of pointers (called molecule by Warren [Warren 77]): one points to a goal's source term; another one points to the goal's frame. For example, in Figure 7.6 (a), **fap** and **fbp** are pointers to frames **fa** and **fb** respectively. The goals in the *and* queue may have different frames as shown in Figure 7.6(a), because they may be from different clauses.

The environment refers to all the frames in the node. A frame contains a set for value cells of variables which occur in one clause. Its structure is shown in Figure 7.6(b). The value of a variable can be classified into several types which were described in Section 6.2.1. Unlike the traditional implementation method, a new data type, named *or-shared* variable and formed (**shared** : i/p), is introduced. This means the variable has multiple local values kept in a hash table p and the most senior local binding is currently not higher than the i-generation node.

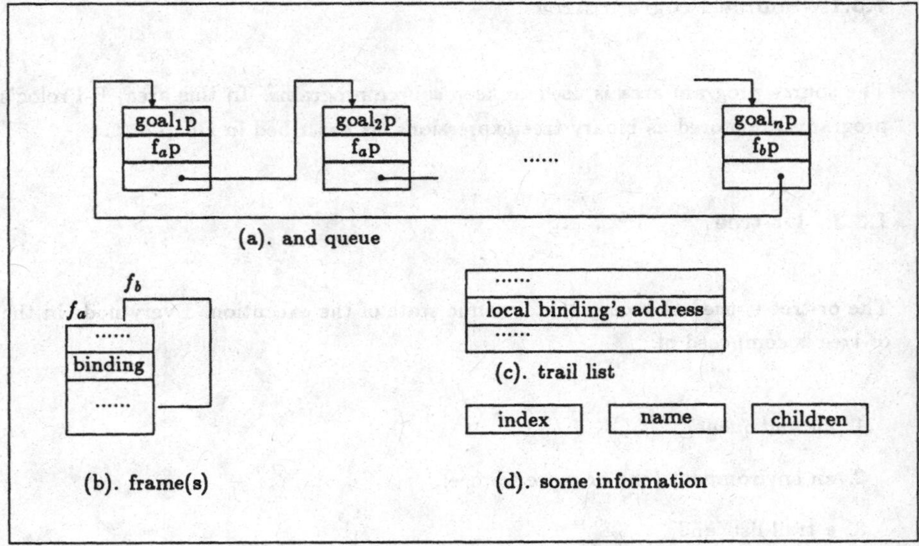

Figure 7.6 Composition of a Node

The trail list is used to keep all the addresses of or-shared variables' bindings which occurred while executing this node's goals.

The node's information includes the following data: number of the node's children (called **children**), index of the node and name of the node. (The meaning of a node's index and name are defined in Chapter 6.)

7.3.3 Hash Table

Every or-shared variable has a hash table. The hash table is constituted like Figure 7.7 (also refer to Figure 6.11). **count** is the current number of bindings in the table. **home** is the index of a node in which the or-shared variable's *global cell* is (see Def 6.1 for *global cell*). For example, in Figure 7.5, or-shared variable **A**'s **home** is 0, and **count** is 3 and 2 at step 3 and step 4 respectively. The column **binding** keeps the local bindings, and the column **key** keeps the node names corresponding to each local binding.

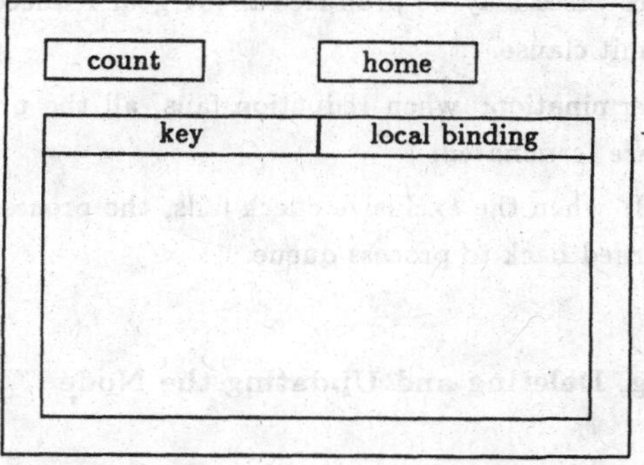

Figure 7.7 Hash Table

7.4 The Or-tree Model

Conventionally, the tree models such as or-tree, and-tree and and-or-tree are regarded as a process tree, in which the nodes are processes (or-processes or and-processes), and only leaf nodes are treated as runnable processes. The or-tree model to be presented in this dissertation is completely different in this sense. For our or-tree, a node in the tree is not a process, but a set of processes. And not only leaf nodes but also non-leaf nodes are runnable.

7.4.1 Node

As noted in Section 7.3, there is an and-queue in the node. In fact, an element of an and-queue is regarded as a process descriptor, so the and-queue can be regarded as a process queue. Here, a process in our scheme is defined as:

1. process = a goal's code +this goal's frame
2. to run a process means to reduce its goal.
3. running a process can cause three kinds of results as follows:

- successful termination: when reduction succeeds, the process is terminated. (new processes may be produced if the goal reduced to other goals, using a non-unit clause.
- failed termination: when reduction fails, all the processes in the process queue are terminated.
- suspend: when the exclusive check fails, the process is suspended. It will be returned back to process queue.

7.4.2 Creating, Deleting and Updating the Node

Some new words used from this section are explained first.

Definition 7.1 current node: The node being processed at the moment is called *current node.*

Definition 7.2 home node: the concept of *home node* relates to an or-shared variable. As mentioned in Section 6.2, every or-shared variable has a global cell. We call the node in which the or-shared variable's global cell is the *home node* of this or-shared variable.

Definition 7.3 Communicator: An or-shared variable is regarded as a communicator in the following cases:

1. If an or-shared variable's *home node* is the same as the *current node*, we call the or-shared variable a *communicator.*
2. If an or-shared variable has some local bindings in the nodes below *current node*, we also call it *communicator.*

For example, in Figure 7.8, after step 2, variable **X** becomes an or-shared variable. Then, at step 3, when goal **h(X)** is unified, variable **X** is regarded as a communicator, because **X**'s home node is *N* and current node is also *N. Communicators* play an important role in communication between goals which may have multiple local bindings.

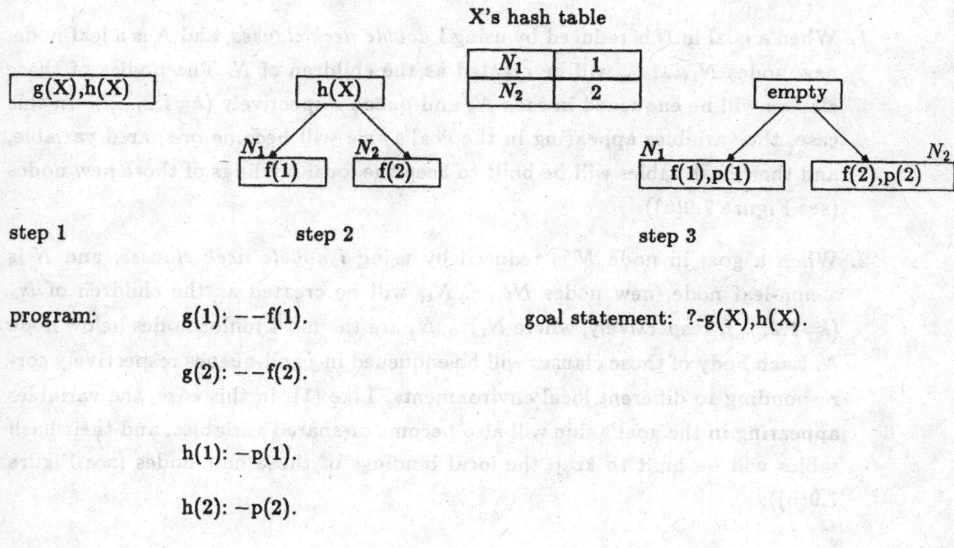

Figure 7.8 An Example for Explaining Communicator

Definition 7.4 multiple reduction: When reducing a goal containing at least one *communicator* variable, we should use all local bindings, which belong to the *current node*, kept in the *communicators'* hash tables to unify with the goal. Therefore, we may obtain more than one result of reduction. This case is called *multiple reduction.*

(1) Creating Node

A root N_0 is created when we try to execute a goal clause (goal statement). All the goals in the clause are enqueued in the and-queue, with the statement's frame.

From a node N, new nodes may be created only when a goal in node N is reduced by using a number i *double neck clauses* ($i > 1$). There are two different ways of creating nodes according to two different cases:

1. When a goal in N is reduced by using i *double neck clauses*, and N is a leaf node, new nodes $N_1, ..., N_i$ will be created as the children of N. The bodies of those clauses will be enqueued in each N_k and-queue respectively (k=1,2,...,i). In this case, the variables appearing in the goal's side will become or-shared variable, and their hash tables will be built to keep the local bindings of those new nodes (see Figure 7.9(a)).

2. When a goal in node N is reduced by using i *double neck clauses*, and N is a non-leaf node, new nodes $N_{k1}, ..., N_{ki}$ will be created as the children of N_k (k=1,2,...,j) respectively, where $N_1, ..., N_j$ are the most junior nodes below node N. Each body of those clauses will be enqueued in j and-queues respectively corresponding to different local environments. Like (1), in this case, the variables appearing in the goal's side will also become or-shared variables, and their hash tables will be built to keep the local bindings of those new nodes (see Figure 7.9(b)).

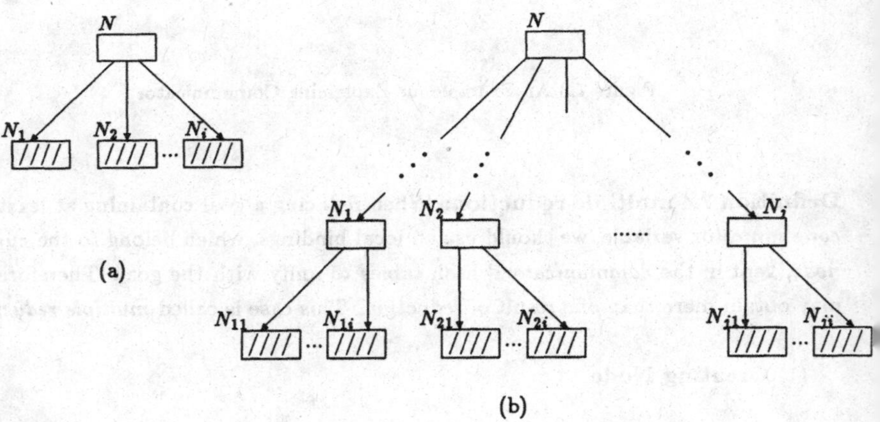

N: current node

Shaded Node: new created node

Figure 7.9 Creating Node

(2) Deleting Node

A node N_1 may be deleted in the following cases:

1. When a goal in a leaf node N_1 fails in reduction, N_1 will be deleted. At this time, the **children** of N_1's father must be decreased by one.
2. If a goal in non-leaf node N_1 fails in reduction, N_1 and all the successors of N_1 will be deleted. Also **children** of the father of N_1 must be decreased by one.
3. After a node N_1's **children** is reduced to zero, N_1 will be deleted, and its father's **children** must be decreased by one too.

The three cases above occur when a process is terminated in failing. That is to say, we only delete the node due to a failure. It also needs to be mentioned that when a node is going to be deleted, variables in the trail list must be reset to unbound.

(3) Updating Node

Here, the exact meaning of updating a node does not mean to update a node but a node's and-queue.

An and-queue may be updated after reduction: the reduced goal is removed from the queue, and the new goals may be introduced into the queue. Some different cases of updating are summarized as following:

dequeue: after a goal succeeds in unification, the goal is dequeued.

enqueue: there are two cases of enqueue:

- As mentioned above, if a goal can be reduced to more than one *double neck* clause, new nodes will be created. On the other hand, when the clause reduced is a *single neck* clause or just one *double neck* clause, it is not necessary to create new nodes. We only put the body (if it exists) into the and-queue of the current node or in an and-queue of a successor according to the following rules:

  1. If no communicator appears, the body is enqueued in the current node's and-queue.

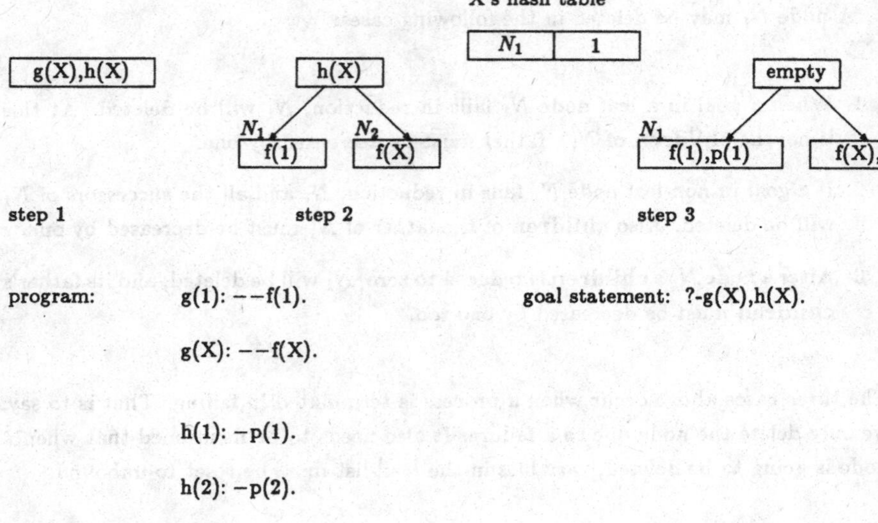

Figure 7.10 An Example of Goal-drop

2. If at least one communicator appears, the body is enqueued in successor nodes' and-queues according to the communicator's hash table.

- Suppose a goal needs a *multiple reduction* (see Def. 7.4), and all solutions have not collected completely yet (see Section 7.5 about how to test whether all solutions have collected). In this case, the goal is dequeued as usual, but also enqueued in the most senior nodes whose local value of the communicator is still unbound. We call this case *goal-drop*. Figure 7.10 is an example of *goal-drop*. At step 3 of Figure 7.10, because **X** has only one local binding of node N_1, **h(X)** is dropped down to the node N_2.

7.4.3 The Relation Between the Nodes

In the or-tree model, the relation between the nodes is as shown in Figure 7.11. The relation between any node and its brother is *or*. The relation between one node and its ancestor or successor, namely the nodes in the same path, is *and*. That is to say,

a node's process queue is shared by all of its children.

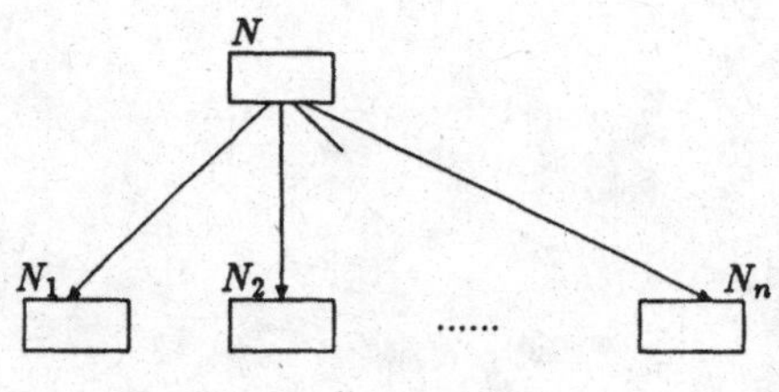

N and (N_1 or N_2 or ... or N_n)

= (N and N_1) or (N and N_2) or ... or (N and N_n)

Figure 7.11 Relation Between the Or-tree's Nodes

Every node can be executed provided that its process queue is not empty.

The conditions terminating all the executions are:

success: **If there exists one path in the tree all of whose and-queues are empty, the execution is stopped. (It can be re-started to search for other solutions automatically or manually.)**

failure: **If root is deleted.**

7.4.4 Examples

(1) A Words Translator

First, we give an example which does not include or-parallelism.

Program 7.1 **a one-to-one translator**

(1) start: – in_stream(X), look_up(X,Y).

```
(2) look_up([H1|S1],[H2|S2]): - trans(H1,H2),
                    look_up(S1,S2).
(3) look_up([ ],[ ]).

(4) trans(1,one).
(5) trans(2,two).
(6) trans(3,three).
            :
            :
            :
```

(refer to Program 4.3 for **in_stream**)

This program only has a single producer and a single consumer. The execution of ?- **start** with input stream [1,2,......] is shown in Figure 7.12. In this figure (also Figure 7.13 and 7.15), the goal marked by underline will be reduced at the next step. Because Program 7.1 does not include or-parallelism, the or-tree will never be extended, that is, all the processes belong to the root node.

The next program includes a single stream producer and multiple consumers.

Program 7.2 a one-to-many translator

(**start, look_up** and **in_stream** are same as in Program 7.1)

```
(1) trans(sweet,amai): --true.
(2) trans(sweet,oishii): --true.
(3) trans(sweet,yasashii): --true.
(4) trans(hot,atsui): --true.
(5) trans(hot,karai): --true.
(6) trans(hot,hageshii): --true.
(7) trans(warm,atatakai): --true.
(8) trans(warm,nessin): --true.
(9) trans(warm,omoiyarigaaru): --true.
            :
            :
            :
```

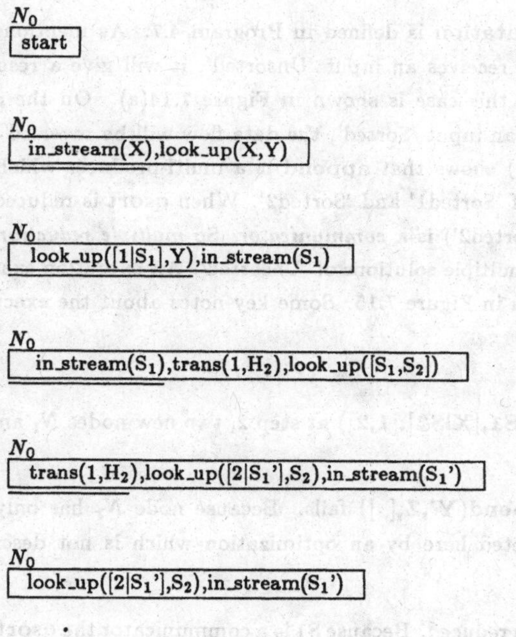

Figure 7.12 Execution Procedure of Program 7.1

The execution of ?- **start** with input stream [sweet,warm,......] is shown in Figure 7.13. The difference between this program and Program 7.2 is that **trans** is defined by *double necks* clauses. Therefore, after the **trans** goal is reduced, the or-tree should be expanded, and the hash table is built. Finally, this program will produce multiple streams of **Y**.

(2) Sort and Permutation

Program **sort and permutation** is defined in Program 4.7. As mentioned in Section 4.3.2, if this program receives an input 'Unsorted', it will give a result of sorted list. The data flow of this case is shown in Figure 7.14(a). On the other hand, if we give this program an input 'Sorted', the data flow will be reversed as in Figure 7.14(b). Figure 7.14(b) shows that **append** is a multi-producer which can produce more than one pair of 'Sorted1' and 'Sorted2'. When **qsort** is reduced, we can find that 'Sorted1' (or 'Sorted2') is a *communicator*. So *multiple reduction* will occur. Lastly, we can obtain multiple solutions of 'Unsorted'. An execution example of ?- **qsort(R,[1,2])** is shown in Figure 7.15. Some key notes about the execution example are as follows:

1. After reducing **append(S1,[X|S2],[1,2])** at step 2, two new nodes N_1 and N_2 are created.
2. At step 4, reducing **append(Y',Z,[ ])** fails. Because node N_2 has only one successor N_3, N_3 is deleted here by an optimization which is not described above.
3. At step 5, **qsort(S,S1)** is reduced. Because S1 is a communicator the **qsort(S,S1)** is multiply reduced.

7.5 Some Notes on Implementation

In our practical implementation at this moment, we use the method described in Section 6.3 to manage the or-tree and hash tables. The nodes in the tree are named by Formula 6.1.

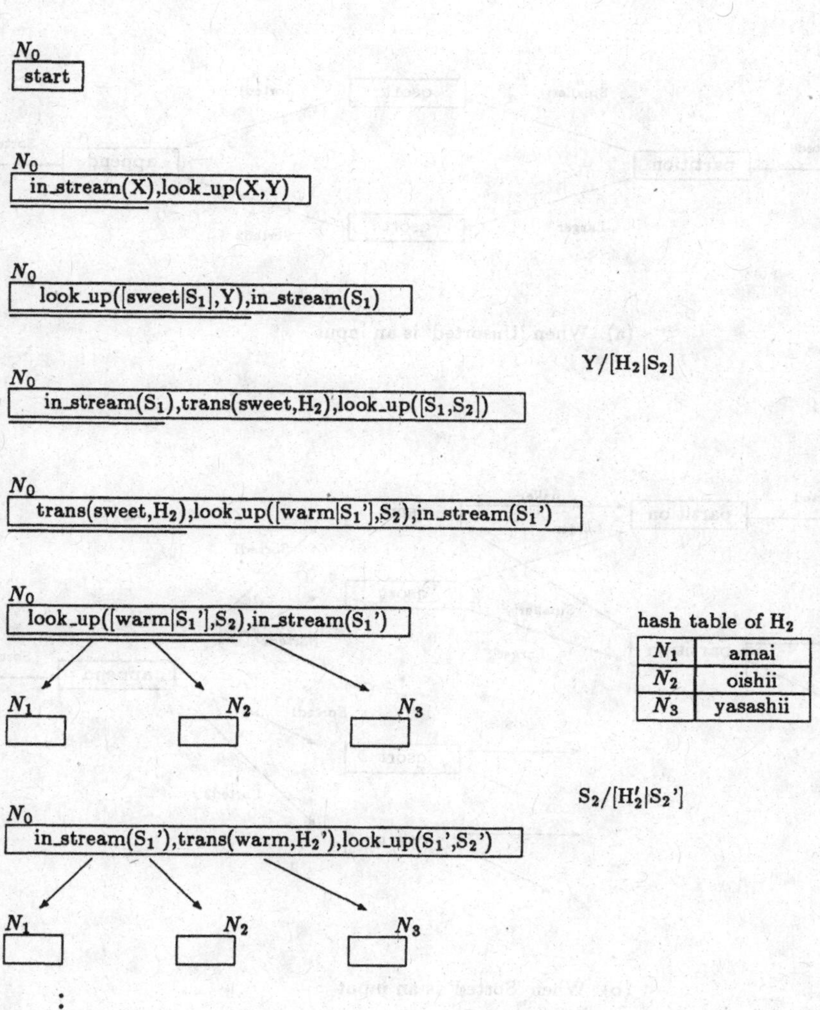

Figure 7.13 Execution Procedure of Program 7.2

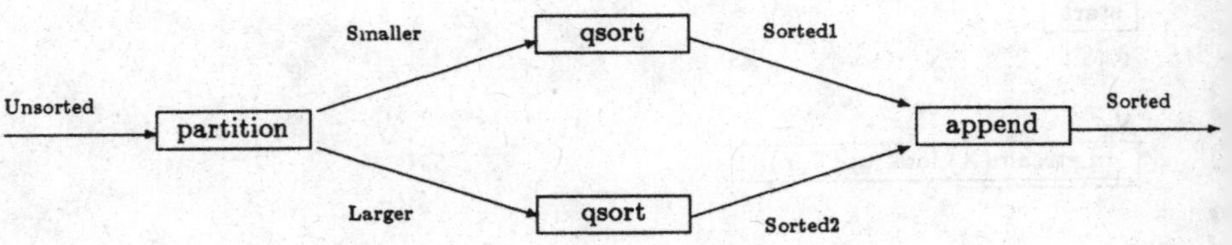

(a). When 'Unsorted' is an input

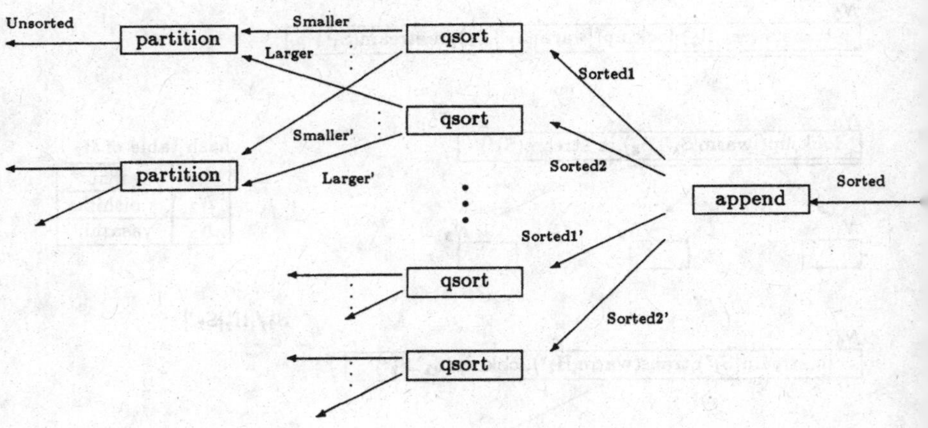

(b). When 'Sorted' is an input

Figure 7.14 The Data Flow of Program 4.7

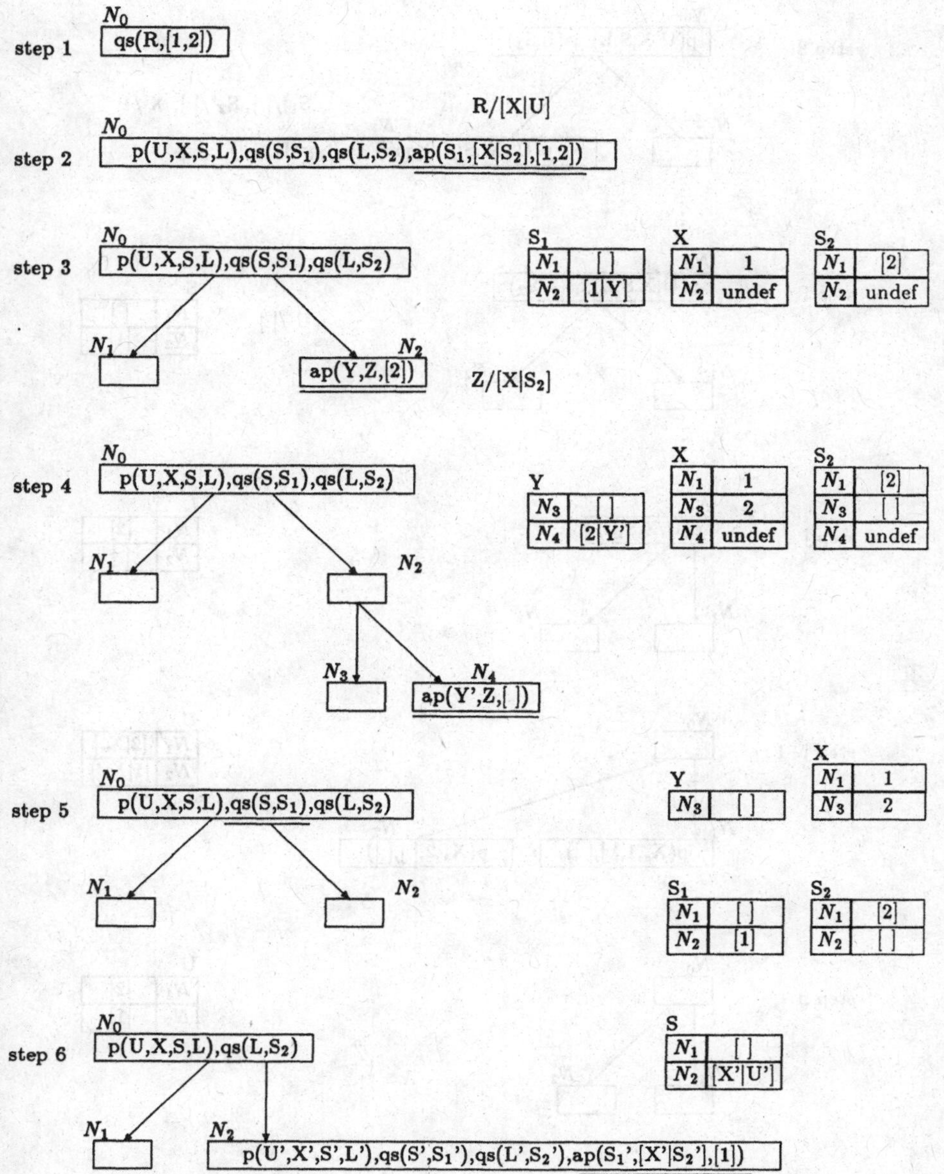

Figure 7.15 (1) Execution Procedure of Program 4.7

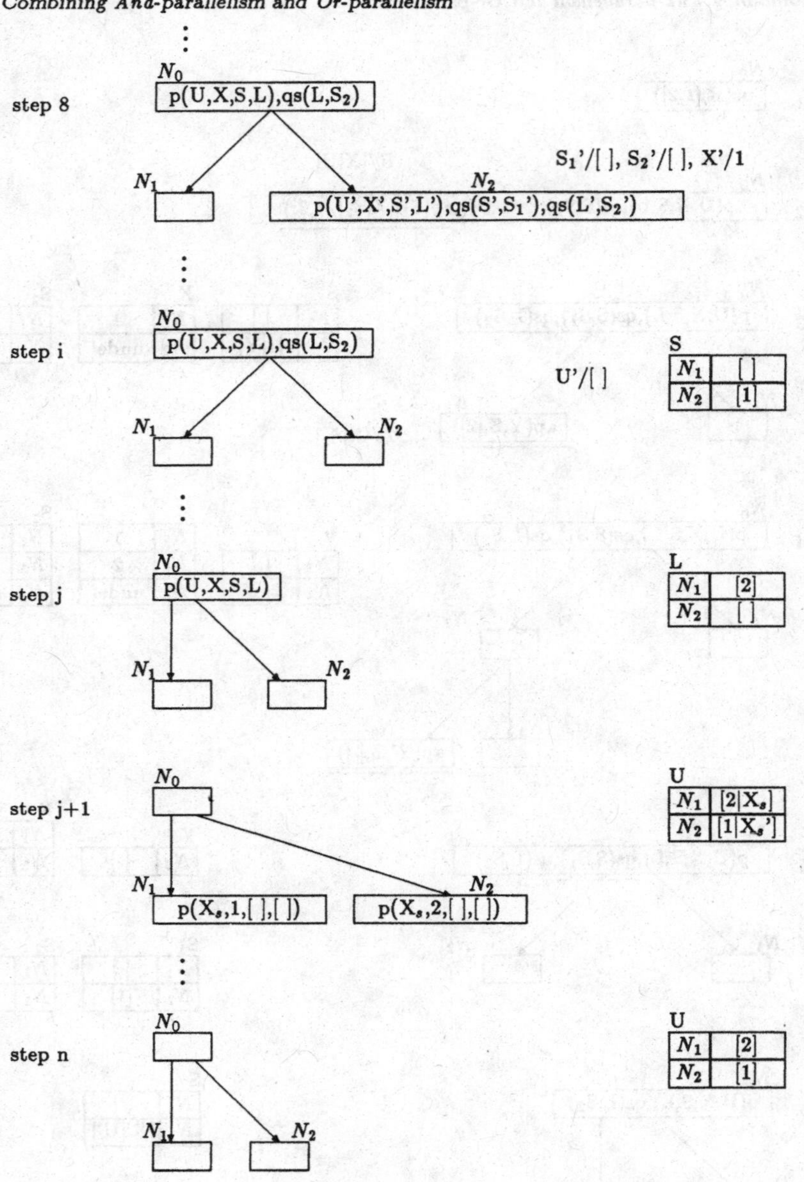

Figure 7.15 (2) Execution Procedure of Program 4.7

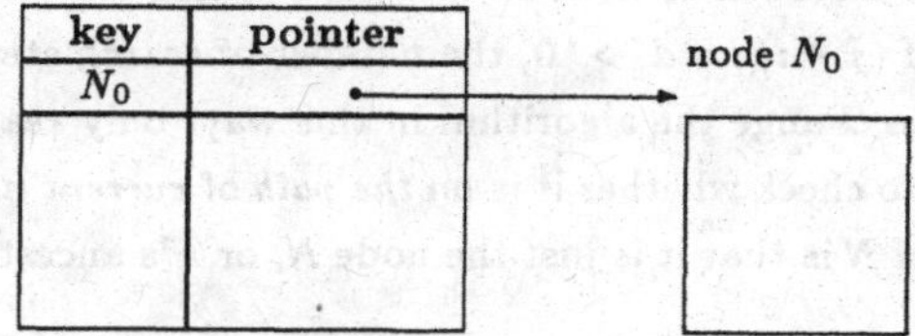

Figure 7.16 Or-tree Table

For tree processing, an or-tree table is used to keep the node items. The or-tree table is constructed like Figure 7.16. The column **key** keeps the nodes' names, and the column **pointer** keeps the pointers which point to the corresponding nodes. Clearly, by using this table, it is very simple to search, create and delete a node in the tree provided that we have the node's name. The main problem in implementation is how to process or-shared variables during unification. Three things must be explained here:

1. How to know whether an or-shared variable is a communicator or not.
2. How to find out all local bindings of an or-shared variable.
3. How to proceed if an or-shared variable is a communicator.

According to Definition 7.3, we can see that there are two different cases of communicator. If the *current node* has the same index as the or-shared variable's *home node*, we know this or-shared variable is a communicator immediately. Otherwise, it can be checked during looking up the local binding(s).

As discussed in Section 6.2 and 6.3, we can use the algorithm which is similar to Figure 6.4 and the method for computing the node's name to search for the local bindings efficiently. There is also an optimum method which can be used when

$$\text{count} < (j - i)$$

where the **count** is the current number of bindings in the hash table, j is an *index* of *current node* and i is the most senior node's *index* kept in this hash table. In Section 6.2 we mentioned that if $(j - i) = d > 0$, the number of search steps will be $o(\mathrm{d})$. But if d <**count**, we can change the algorithm in this way: only reading the node's names kept in the table to check whether it is *on the path* of *current node* or not. The meaning of *on the path* of *N* is that it is just the node *N*, or *N*'s ancestor or successor.

Three kinds of result of looking up the local binding are as follows:

1. There is no binding which belongs to the *current node*. In this case, the or-shared variable's local value will be regarded as an unbound variable.
2. There is a binding whose node is the *current node* or an ancestor of the *current node*. In this case, the or-shared variable's local value will be regarded as this binding.
3. Otherwise, the binding(s) found are successor(s) of the *current node*. In this case, the or-shared variable will be regarded as a *communicator*.

The method of processing a communicator is explained below. It is not difficult to process if all the bindings have been collected in the hash table. The only thing we should do is to reduce the goal using all the bindings, and put the different results of reduction into its binding's node (if single neck) or create new nodes below the binding's node (if double neck). The rather complicated problem is how to process a special case named *goal-drop* (see Section 7.4.2).

First, we must give an efficient method for testing whether the local bindings have collected completely or not. A simple example shown in Figure 7.17 is used to explain. Suppose an or-shared variable **X** has three local bindings which are bound at nodes N_1, N_2, N_3 respectively, but for node M_2, there has been no value produced for **X** yet. If **X**'s hash table is like Table 1 in Figure 7.17, it will be difficult to test. We must look up the **children** number of the father of N_1, N_2, N_3 first. Then, **children** = 3 tells us that the local bindings below node M_1 are all collected. Next, we must look up the **children** number of the father of M_1. At this time, **children** = 2 tells us that there are some bindings not collected yet. Clearly, this method is very inefficient, so we are not using it.

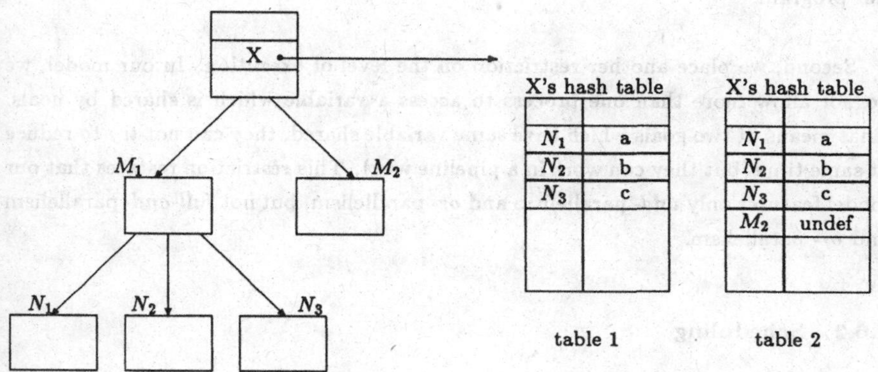

Figure 7.17 An Optimization of Hash Table Management

A more efficient method is the following. The hash table is built like Table 2 rather than Table 1, so that we can know that node M_2 has no local bindings immediately without any searching like the above. Therefore, what we should do while creating a hash table is to make an entry for 'undef' variable in the hash table for the purpose of testing all solutions efficiently. An entry like 'M_2 : undef' shown in Figure 7.17 will be deleted provided that a successor of M_2 makes a local binding to **X**. Using this method, we can not only know whether all bindings have been collected according to if an 'undef' entry exists, but also can know into which node the goal should be *dropped* down to according to the node names in the 'undef' entries.

7.6 Discussion

7.6.1 Some restrictions

There are two restrictions in our implementation.

First, we place a restriction on the syntax of P-Prolog, that is, recursively defined goals are forbidden from appearing in the guard. Clearly, the reason of this restriction is in order to obtain efficiency. We call a P-Prolog program with this restriction a *flat* program.

Second, we place another restriction on the level of execution. In our model, we do not allow more than one process to access a variable which is shared by goals. That means, if two goals which have same variable shared, they can not try to reduce at same time (but they can work in a pipeline way). This restriction restates that our model features only *and*- parallelism and *or*- parallelism, but not *full-and*- parallelism and *or*- parallelism.

7.6.2 Scheduling

The scheduling in our implementation determines:

1. for the or-tree, which node is selected to be processed first, and
2. for an and-queue, which goal is selected to be reduced first.

We did not mention about the scheduling problem above, because we do not want to impose a certain scheduling method on our model. In the prototype implementation of P-Prolog, the scheduling method is bounded depth first for and-queue and depth first for or-tree. A variety of scheduling methods are going to be compared and evaluated. Also, a dynamic changeable scheduling method can be considered.

7.6.3 Optimizations

There are two optimizations which have not applied to our prototype implementation yet. But they might be worth implementing in our opinion.

One is about how to cut down the overhead of the exclusive check at run time. In our prototype implementation, exclusive relation is checked at run time. In fact, we can use an analysis system to analyze P-Prolog's program. Then we can obtain the mode declarations of all the clauses in the program. This kind of analysis system has be implemented for *flat* P-Prolog [Tamura *et al.* 86]. We expect that, by using static analysis, P-Prolog will be implemented more efficiently, and the compiling method of P-Prolog will be able to be developed.

Another optimization is related to the scheduling problem. At this moment, we only use a busy waiting method to process suspension. It can be expected that the technique proposed by [Colmerauer *et al.* 81] will also be used in P-Prolog's implementation. That is, in addition to the and-queue, some special queues are introduced to keep the suspended goals. The goals kept in a queue are waiting for the same variable to be bound. So as the variable becomes bound, all the goals in that queue can be reduced. This optimization can make the scheduling of goals very efficient (it has been used in the SPM [Foster *et al.* 86], FCP and GHC implementation).

7.6.4 Evaluation

Lastly, P-Prolog's implementation method described above is roughly evaluated in respect of efficiency and parallelism.

As for efficiency, we can say that even though the scheme of implementation looks rather complicated, especially compared with committed choice non-deterministic languages, it can be considered to be implemented with reasonable efficiency. This is because the extra overhead in its implementation can be regarded as only the cost of or-shared variable processing and or-tree management. As discussed above, those kinds of processing are not very expensive. If comparing with the implementation schemes which combine *full-and* and *or-* parallelism, our scheme is quite efficient because, according to the or-tree model, a consistency check can be avoided and redundant searches can also be avoided. On the other hand, the built-in predicate **setof** can be implemented quite efficiently, since all the solutions of a variable are collected in one table.

Because the concept of *or-shared variable* and *communicator* are introduced, we can process the communication between goals quite simply. Because we use the node coding method, centralized method and so on, we can speed up the memory management and redeferencing. Also it seems that node sharing (see Figure 7.11) can cut down the overhead of system management. So we can expect that the or-tree model can be executed reasonably efficiently.

As for parallelism, because P-Prolog does not feature *full-and-* parallelism, it loses some parallelism compared with pure Horn clauses. But it has extremely high parallelism compared with committed choice non-deterministic languages.

Chapter 8

Conclusion

8.1 Contributions

The main contributions of this research are a novel parallel logic programming language named P-Prolog and an execution model for combining *and*-parallelism and *or*-parallelism.

As mentioned in Chapter 1 and Chapter 3, the primary goal of this research was to develop a parallel logic language which is more 'complete' and 'logical', that is, transparent to the user without extralogical restrictions. In order to achieve this goal, several efforts are made, and the following results have been obtained.

First, the notion of guarded Horn clauses was extended by introducing the exclusive relation. The extended guarded Horn clause is called the *classified guarded Horn clause*. Based on the *classified guarded Horn clause*, P-Prolog is proposed and developed. The advances included in P-Prolog are:

1. The user can easily write a program without caring about synchronization problems provided that the exclusive relation between clauses are pointed out. Also, the synchronization mechanism in P-Prolog can determine the direction of data flow dynamically.

2. By using *classified guarded Horn clauses*, the user can classify the clauses into *don't care* non-deterministic clauses and *don't know* non-deterministic clauses.

That is to say, P-Prolog can describe *or-* parallelism naturally.

The second result is an execution model which is proposed to implement P-Prolog but is not limited to P-Prolog. The main problem of combining *and-* and *or-* parallelism is not how to express it in the language, but how to implement it efficiently. This means, if we do not support a practical implementation method for P-Prolog, it will only be worth using a subset of P-Prolog which is similar to committed choice non-deterministic languages. Therefore, the more important thing is to find an execution model which can combine *and*-parallelism and *or*-parallelism in a reasonably efficient manner. The or-tree model is presented in this dissertation to solve this problem. Its characteristics can be summarized as:

1. The *or-shared variable* is distinguished from other data types.
2. The *communicator*, a special or-shared variable is defined, by which multiple solutions can be sent out.
3. Every node in the or-tree is shared by its successors. This means that if an or-branch occurs, we do not copy any of the goals and environments, so they can be shared.

Third, a prototype implementation of P-Prolog's interpreter (in C) has been designed and coded.

8.2 Further Work

There are many topics for further research:

1. The implementation scheme of P-Prolog to be developed now is only an interpreter. We should study a compiler for P-Prolog, and design an abstract machine in order to implement it more efficiently.
2. We also must start to study an architecture for P-Prolog or execute it on some existing multi-processor machines. In particularly, the former is very important. As noted in this dissertation, there are many techniques used in P-Prolog that

can be implemented more efficiently provided that some special hardware is supposed, such as BTM and CAM.

3. Because techniques of implementation for committed choice non-deterministic languages are studied successfully, and there are some special machines for them being developed, it is worth researching the translation between P-Prolog and committed choice non-deterministic languages.

Bibliography

[Butler *et al.* 86] R. Butler, E.L. Lusk, R. Olson and R.A. Overbeek, Oct. 1986. 'A Parallel Implementation of the Warren Abstract Machine', *Research Report, Mathematics and Computer Science Division, Argonne National Laboratory*

[Chang and Lee 73] C. Chang and R.C. Lee, 1973. *'Symbolic Logic and Mechanical Theorem Proving'*, Academic Press.

[Ciepielewski 84] A. Ciepielewski, May 1984. 'Towards a computer architecture for or-parallel execution of logic programs'. PhD thesis, *Technical report TRITA-CS-8401,* Dept. of Computer System, Royal Institute of Technology, Stockholm.

[Clark and McCabe 79] K.L. Clark and F.G. McCabe, 1979. 'The control facilities of IC-PROLOG'. In *Expert Systems in the Microelectronic age,* Edinburgh University Press.

[Clark and Gregory 81] K.L. Clark and S. Gregory, Oct. 1981. 'A relational language for parallel programming'. In *Proceedings of the ACM Conference on Functional Programming Languages and Computer Architecture* , pp. 171-178.

[Clark *et al.* 82] K.L. Clark, F.G. McCabe and S. Gregory, 1982. 'IC-PROLOG language features'. In *Logic Programming,* London: Academic Press, pp. 253-266.

[Clark and Gregory 83] K.L. Clark and S. Gregory, May 1983. 'PARLOG: a parallel logic programming language'. *Research report DOC 83/5.* Dept. of Computing, Imperial College, London.

[Clark and Gregory 86] K.L. Clark and S. Gregory, January 1986. 'PARLOG: parallel programming in logic'. In *ACM Transactions on Programming Languages and Systems 8, 1*, pp. 1-49.

[Clomerauer *et al.* 81] A. Colmerauer, H. Kanui and M. van Kaneghem, 1981. 'Last steps towards an ultimate Prolog', In *Proceedings of the Seventh International Joint Conference on Artificial Intelligence*, pp. 947-948. IJCAI.

[Conery 83] J.S. Conery, 1983. 'The AND/OR Process Model for Parallel Execution of Logic Programs', Ph.D. dissertation, University of California, Irvine, *Tech. Report 204*, Information and Computer Science.

[Crammond 85] J. Crammond, Oct. 1985. 'A Comparative Study of Unification Algorithms for OR-Parallel Execution of Logic Languages', In *IEEE transactions on computers, c-34, 10*, pp. 911-917.

[DeGroot 84] D. DeGroot, Nov. 1984. 'Restricted AND-Parallelism', In *Proceedings of the International Conference on Fifth Generation Computer Systems*, pp. 471-478.

[Dijkstra 75] E.W. Dijkstra, Aug. 1975. 'Guarded Commands, nondeterminacy, and formal derivation of programs', In *Commun. ACM 18, 8* pp. 453-457.

[Foster *et al.* 86] I. Foster, S. Gregory, G. Ringwood and K. Satoh, July 1986. 'A Sequential Implementation of PARLOG', In *Proceedings of 3rd International Logic Programming Conference*, pp. 149-156.

[Gregory 86] S. Gregory, 1986-87, *'Parallel Logic Programming in PARLOG'*, Addison-Wesley.

[Hoare 61] C.A.R. Hoare, 1961. 'Algorithm 64', In *CACM, Vol. 4* page 321.

[Hoare 78] C.A.R. Hoare, 1978. 'Communicating Sequential Processes,' In *Comm. ACM 21, 2*, pp. 666-677.

[Kasif *et al.* 83] S.Kasif, M. Kohli and J. Minker, 1983. 'PRISM: a parallel inference system for problem solving', In *Proceedings of the Logic Programming Workshop 83*, pp. 123-152.

[Knuth 68] D. Knuth, 1968. *'The art of computer programming, Vol.1'*, Addison-Wesley.

[Kowalski and Kuehner 71] R.A. Kowalski and D. Kuehner, 1971. 'Linear Resolution with Selection Function', In *Artificial Intelligence Vol. 2*, pp. 227-260.

[Kowalski 79] R.A. Kowalski, 1979. *'Logic for problem solving'*, North-holland.

[Levy 84] J. Levy, July 1984. 'A Unification Algorithm for Concurrent Prolog', In *Proceeding of 2nd International Logic Programming Conference*, pp. 331-343.

[Lindstrom 84] G. Lindstrom, July. 1984. 'Or-parallelism on Applicative Architectures', In *Proceeding of 2nd International Logic Programming Conference*, pp. 159-170.

[Miyazaki et al 85] T. Miyazaki, A. Takeuchi and T. Chikayama, Feb.1985. 'A sequential Implementation of Concurrent Prolog Based on the Shallow Binding Scheme,' In *Proceedings of 1985 International Symposium on Logic Programming*, pp. 110-118.

[Monk 76] J.D. Monk, 1976. *'Mathematical Logic'*, Springer-Verlag.

[Nilsson 80] N.J. Nilsson, 1980. *'Principles of Artificial Intelligence'*, Tioga.

[Okuno 84] H. Okuno, 1984. 'A Problem for 3nd Lisp Contest and 1st Prolog Contest', *IPSJ Working Group Report,* WG-SUM No.28-4.

[Pereira and Nasr 84] L.M. Pereira and R. Nasr, Nov. 1984. 'Delta Prolog: a distributed logic programming language', In *Proceeding of Fifth Generation Computer Systems*, pp. 283-291.

[Pollard 81] G.H. Pollard, 1981. 'Parallel execution of Horn clause programs', Ph.D. thesis, Department of Computing, Imperial College, London.

[Robinson 65] J.A. Robinson, 1965. 'A machine oriented logic based on the resolution principle', In *J. ACM 12, 1*, pp. 23-41.

[Satou *et al.* 84] H. Satou *et al.* 1984. 'A Sequential Implementation of Concurrent Prolog - Based on Deep Binding Scheme', In *The First National Conference of Japan Society for Software Science and Technology.*

[Shapiro 83] E.Y. Shapiro, February 1983. 'A subset of Concurrent Prolog and its interpreter'. *Technical report TR-003*, ICOT, Tokyo.

[Syre and Westphal 85] J. Syre and H. Westphal, June 1985. 'A Review of Parallel Models for Logic Programming languages', *Technical Report CA-07*, European Computer Industry Research Centre, West Germany.

[Tamura *et al.* 86] H. Tamura, R. Yang, Y. Shobatake and H. Aiso, 1986. 'A Debug System for Parallel Logic Programming Language P-Prolog' (in Japanese), In *Spring 86' Conference of Japan Society for Information Processing.*

[Tanaka 86] Tanaka Laboratory, March 1986. 'Status Reports of Highly Parallel Inference Engine PIE'. Dept. of Electrical Eng., Univ. of Tokyo.

[Ueda 85] K. Ueda, September 1985. 'Guarded Horn Clauses', *Technical report TR-103,* ICOT, Tokyo.

[Warren 77] D.H.D. Warren, 1977. 'Implementing Prolog - Compiling Predicate Logic Programs', Research Report No. 39, Dept. of AI, University of Edinburgh.

[Warren 83] D.H.D. Warren, Nov. 1983. 'An Abstract Prolog Instruction Set', Technical Note 309, Artificial Intelligence Center, SRI International.

[Warren 84] D.S. Warren, Feb. 1984, 'Efficient Prolog Memory Management for Flexible Control Strategies', In *Proceedings of 1984 International Symposium on Logic Programming*, pp. 198-202.

[Wos *et al.* 65] L. Wos, G.A. Robinson and D.F. Carson, 1965. 'Efficiency and Completeness of the Set of Support Strategy in Theorem Proving,' In *J. ACM 12, 4*, pp. 536-541.

[Wulf *et al.* 81] W.A. Wulf, M. Show and P.N. Hilfinger, 1981. *'Fundamental Structures of Computer Science'*, Addison-Wesley.

[Yang *et al.* 86a] R. Yang, Y. Shobatake and H. Aiso, Jan. 1986. 'Prolog Machine Based on Binary Tree Memory' In *Proc. of 9th Hawaii Inter. Conf. on System Sciences*, Vol. 1, pp.1-8.

[Yang *et al.* 86b] R. Yang, Y. Shobatake and H. Aiso, July 1986. 'Binary Tree Memory for Prolog System' (in Japanese), In *Journal of IFIP* Vol. 27, pp. 724-734.

[Yang and Aiso 86] R. Yang and H. Aiso, July 1986. 'P-Prolog: A Parallel Logic Language Based on Exclusive Relation', In *Proc. of 3rd International Logic Programming Conference*, pp. 255-269.

Index